Contents

Part 1
Introduction

The life and works of J. D. Salinger

Jerome David Salinger was born in New York on 1 January 1919. His father, Solomon S. Salinger, born in 1888, had moved to New York from Chicago in 1912. His mother, Marie Jillich, changed her name to Miriam on her marriage into a Jewish Family.

Sol Salinger became successful as an importer of cheese but his only son showed no interest in joining the business. It seems, too, that father and son were never close and that the boy was more attached to his mother who may have earlier in life been an actress.

The history of the Salinger family is one of increasing prosperity and the city of New York that is depicted in J. D. Salinger's writings is largely the parts of town which he came to know as a boy. Such landmarks as Central Park Zoo and the Natural History Museum were on his doorstep and constituted his playgrounds. Like his most famous creation, Salinger was a well-off city boy.

Academically Salinger was undistinguished. He attended Manhattan's McBurney school and, at the age of fifteen, was sent as a boarder to Valley Forge Military Academy at Wayne, Pennsylvania. The school had been founded in 1928 with the aim of producing 'young men fully prepared to meet their responsibilities, alert in mind, sound in body, considerate to others, and with a high sense of duty, honor, loyalty and courage. Valley Forge implements these goals and gives them structure through the values found in military discipline'. This was probably the school that gave him the model for Pencey Prep in *The Catcher in the Rye*.

In spite of being enrolled as a boy soldier, Salinger does not seem to have been unhappy at the school. It was here that he began to regard himself as a future professional writer, though none of the apprentice pieces of those years is known to exist with the exception of a class song composed in 1936. This can still be found in the school's hymn book.

In 1936 Salinger was accepted by New York University, but he remained there for a short time only. In late 1937 and early 1938 he visited Europe for five months, partly to improve his German and French. As he spent most of his time in Vienna it is very possible that he witnessed examples of Nazi aggression then commonplace in Austria. On his return to America he enrolled in Ursinus, a small liberal arts college at a place called Collegeville in Pennsylvania. He was then nineteen years old.

After only one term at Ursinus he took an evening class in short-story writing at Columbia University, New York and his serious apprenticeship in the craft began. His teacher was Whit Burnett, editor of *Story* magazine, and it was this magazine which published Salinger's first story, 'The Young Folks', originally written as a class exercise. It appeared in the March-April 1940 issue, an occasion that may be taken as the beginning of Salinger's career as a professional writer. He was paid a fee of twenty-five dollars for it.

He next published a story entitled 'Go See Eddie' in the *University of Kansas City Review* and another, 'The Hang of It', in *Colliers*. In November 1941 Salinger achieved an ambition when he sold 'Slight Rebellion off Madison' to *The New Yorker*. The publication of this story was delayed by the war. Its chief interest to readers today is that it seems to have been Holden Caulfield's first appearance in fiction.

The United States entered the Second World War in December 1941 following the Japanese attack on the US fleet at the naval base in Pearl Harbour, in the Hawaiian islands. Salinger was drafted into the army in the following April and in late 1943 he was transferred into the recently formed Counter Intelligence Corps. He saw service at Utah Beach in Normandy during the D-Day invasion, June 1944; he was involved at the battle of Hürtgen Forest later that year and was a part of the battle for Luxembourg in December 1944.

It has been rumoured that Salinger suffered some form of nervous collapse as a result of these wartime experiences. It is also reported that during these various engagements he kept his typewriter with him and wrote when ever he had an opportunity.

In 1945 he married a French doctor, but the marriage lasted only eight months and, on her return home to France after a visit to the States, his wife obtained a divorce.

In 1946 *The New Yorker* accepted a ninety-five page manuscript about Holden Caulfield, but it was never printed.

A story published in 1947 called 'The Inverted Forest' is of interest because the central character, Ray Ford, seems to be a prototype for the Seymour Glass in 'A Perfect Day for Bananafish' which was published in *The New Yorker* on 31 January 1948. The importance of this story is that it is the first to reveal something of the range of Salinger's talent, a talent that would make him one of the most celebrated writers of the post Second World War generation. The novelist, John Updike, has written that it was 'in Salinger that I first heard, as a college student in the early fifties, the tone that spoke to my condition'. He added that the 'stories as they appeared in *The New Yorker* . . . seemed to me to say something about the energies of people and the ways they encountered each other that I did not find in the stories of Hemingway or John O'Hara or Dorothy Parker or any of that "wised-up" style of short-story writing'.

Later in 1948 *The New Yorker* published 'Uncle Wiggily in Connecticut' and 'Just Before the War with the Eskimos', and, in 1949, 'The Laughing Man'. In the same year 'Down in the Dinghy' appeared in the April issue of *Harper's*. In 1950 *The New Yorker* carried the now famous story, 'For Esmé – With Love and Squalor' and, in July 1951, 'Pretty Mouth and Green My Eyes'. Two days after the latter story appeared, on 16 July 1951, the Boston publisher, Little, Brown, released the first copies of *The Catcher in the Rye*.

With stories published in prestigious journals such as the *Saturday Evening Post*, *Esquire* and *The New Yorker*, Salinger was by this time thought to be a writer of considerable promise. However, none of his stories had prepared the literary world for his novel 'about this kid in New York during the Christmas holidays'. It became a huge success in the United States, though it was to be another five years before the novel achieved its cult status with young readers in America and eventually throughout much of the world.

At one point in the novel Holden Caulfield advises any reader who enjoys a book to pick up a telephone and call the author. In view of this it is ironic that Salinger has spent more than forty years avoiding such contacts from appreciative readers of his works as well as the attentions of literary journalists and critics. He is that most un-American phenomenon, a writer who has become famous for not wanting to be famous. A clue to this almost obsessive self-protection may be found in the reaction of Seymour Glass, one of Salinger's characters, to a reading of Flaubert's letters. Seymour observes that the correspondence is so good that it represents waste of a heartbreaking kind. From this we may assume that Salinger, like his fictional creation, passionately believes that nothing should get in the way of his art, especially the by-roads of celebrity.

Following *The Catcher in the Rye* a selection of short works entitled *Nine Stories* was published in April 1953. In Britain it was released with the title *For Esmé – With Love and Squalor, and Other Stories*, a title that Salinger had refused to allow when first suggested a few months earlier.

In January 1955 *The New Yorker* published 'Franny' and in May 1957 'Zooey' appeared in the same journal. In 1961 these two novellas were published as a book entitled *Franny and Zooey*. These works continued Salinger's obsession with the Glass family, a husband and wife vaudeville team and their seven children. This family was a fictional invention which, according to Ian Hamilton, afforded the author 'a means of exploring his own separate selves'.

Two long Glass family stories, 'Raise High the Roof Beams, Carpenters' and 'Seymour: An Introduction', were published in one volume in 1963. On the dustjacket of that book there was a suggestion that more Glass stories were on the way; they have still not arrived and many readers suspect that Salinger has exhausted the potential of that particular family. His most recent story entitled 'Hapworth 16, 1924' appeared as long ago as June 1965 and was published in *The New Yorker*.

Salinger now lives in Cornish, New Hampshire and guards his privacy. He does not give interviews and has long ago insisted that biographical details and the customary photography of the author should not appear on any of his books. In 1986 he was forced to break cover in order to prevent the publication of a biography by the English critic, Ian Hamilton. Salinger's success in preventing the publication of this work led Hamilton to write *In Search of J. D. Salinger* (1988). This book constitutes a substantial literary biography as well as being a fascinating enquiry into the nature of the biographer's art.

The Catcher in the Rye and American society

Salinger's early fiction, including *The Catcher in the Rye*, reflects the period of post-war reconstruction in the United States of America. The end of the Second World War, hastened by the atomic bombs that laid waste the Japanese cities of Hiroshima and Nagasaki, saw the United States emerge as the most powerful nation on earth. Nevertheless, much of the rest of the world was resistant to this domination. In a world fragmented and dislocated by the conflict of 1939–45, the Soviet Union and the USA were to vie for power and influence for the duration of what came to be called 'the Cold War'. The mood of the times that was generated by the superpowers found expression in Winston Churchill's speech at Fulton, Missouri on 5 March 1946. He addressed President Truman, sitting at his side, and the world at large saying that 'from Stettin in the Baltic to Trieste in the Adriatic, an iron curtain has descended across the continent'. Churchill's histrionic warning that Russia was intent upon destroying western civilisation matched perfectly the mood of American domestic politics.

America's preoccupation with what became popularly known as 'red fascism' was deepened by President Truman's order of March 1947 that investigations be made into the loyalty of more than 3 million employees of the government. The emergence of Senator Joseph R. McCarthy in 1950 as the most virulent anti-communist 'witch-hunter' marked the cynical manipulation of a growing hysteria. That this largely illusory communist threat that led to the ruin of so many careers and family lives should have so preoccupied the most powerful nation on earth is indicative of the extent to which the USA was unsure of its present state and future direction in the immediate post-war years.

The end of the war, coming sooner than government planners had expected, left most Americans pessimistic about the future. Cutbacks in the production of wartime goods caused massive lay-offs and the ranks of the unemployed were swelled by discharged servicemen. There was, too, a widespread feeling that the conclusion of the war had not seen the beginning of peace. Indeed, there was an ever-present fear of nuclear holocaust which was increased by America's engagement in war against North Korea (1950–53).

In order to counter the economic situation and the prevailing mood of gloom, the Truman administration set about creating full employment and expanded the New Deal programmes of the 1930s. The relative prosperity of the war years had resulted in high levels of savings and, in spite of the unemployment figures in the mid-1940s, there was no danger of another depression like that of the previous decade. Indeed, the US economy, after a short period of readjustment, was to experience a quarter-century of unexpected boom. This was to result in a society of unprecedented prosperity in the developed world, marked by growth in consumer goods, the spread of education and health care as well as major improvements in transport throughout the United States and the rest of the world.

Perhaps the most visible manifestation of this progress was the spread of home ownership and the shift of a large part of the urban population to the new suburbs. Cheap and efficient housing was made possible by the mass-produced tract houses designed by William Levitt. The construction of Levittown, Long Island, was to be a model for much suburban development in the 1950s. The move to the suburbs was to a great extent the result of changing notions about the American family and the desire for material comfort that characterised the postwar middle classes. The so-called 'babyboom' that began in about 1946 reflected a growing confidence in the American way of life that was accompanied by a decline in both city dwelling and the family farm. All these factors contributed to the popularity of suburban living with its increased space, the absence of city noise and smells and the feeling of being closer to nature. These suburbs constituted communities with shared assumptions and aspirations. Typically, they were made up of young parents with small children who enjoyed shared experiences and comparable incomes. They commuted to work and the sense of community was cemented by such things as car pools and family leisure activities. This way of life led to an ideology of family togetherness and the rigid casting of male and female roles. The image of the typical happy family such as the one portrayed in the popular television series *Father Knows Best* (1954–63) was promoted and reinforced in innumerable Hollywood movies of the late 1940s and 1950s.

Inevitably such cultural and economic shifts in American life had their casualties. Women, many of whom had responsible jobs during the war years, were pressured into fitting the image of wife, homemaker and mother. Such women came under the powerful spell of Dr Benjamin Spock's *Baby and Child Care* (1946) and were encouraged always to subsume their own needs to those of their children; to many women the home became a kind of prison. The substantial number of women who joined the workforce either from choice or economic necessity tended to get jobs with lower pay and lower status than their male counterparts.

The image of a nation rebuilding its economy and social fabric in the late 1940s was seriously tarnished by the many poor and dispossessed who were not middle-class or white or suburbanite. These years constituted a period of growing power for African-Americans. Politicians such as President Truman and Thomas Dewey, the governor of New York, saw the moral as well as the political need for the extension of civil rights. However, there were strong forces of resistance to all such initiatives in the Republican party and among many Southern democrats who secretly condoned the activities of the Ku Klux Klan. In spite of the president's 1948 special message to Congress that the protection of citizens' rights was 'the duty of every government which derives its power from the consent of the governed', it was to take many years and innumerable small legal and legislative victories before this ideal came even close to realisation. In fact Truman's successor as president in 1952, General Dwight D. Eisenhower, was less than enthusiastic about addressing the need for civil rights legislation. To many the avuncular figure of the war hero-president symbolised the growing complacency of American cultural and political life with its thinly concealed fears of internal subversion and external attacks. This period is remembered as being both repressive and anaesthetised, marked by the collapse of radical politics.

Although *The Catcher in the Rye* pre-dates the Eisenhower years, it was the isolationism, consumerism, conformity and apathy of that era that the novel seemed to capture for a later generation of readers in the 1950s and the 1960s. Politically and culturally the 1960s are different from the decade that preceded them and it is ironic that it was to be the 'babyboomers' of postwar suburbia who would respond most deeply to the plight of Holden Caulfield. It was that generation to whom *The Catcher in the Rye* spoke most eloquently.

A note on the text

These notes are based on the 1994 Penguin edition of *The Catcher in the Rye* which reproduces the original American version published by Little, Brown of Boston in 1951.

An earlier British version was also published by Hamish Hamilton of London in 1951 and subsequently in paperback by Penguin. It contained about 800 textual changes – most of them minor accommodations of spelling, punctuation and changes in the author's use of italic. Hamish Hamilton's pruning of Salinger's manuscript was obviously an attempt to remove the rough edges of what was a first novel, and to tailor it for a British readership. Salinger must have given Hamish Hamilton freedom to make changes to the original manuscript. We know that the novelist considered his London publisher to be a cut above his American counterpart. Until recently this 1951 British version was the only one available in Britain.

However, in 1994, the original American text was published in Britain for the first time (in hardback by Hamish Hamilton and paperback by Penguin Books).

While, in 1951, Hamish Hamilton may have expunged some of the italics to make the book easier to read, this new publication of the original text shows how Salinger used italics to suggest the inflections of the narrator's voice – often emphasising the speaker's 'phoniness' and vapid enthusiasm: '*Hol*lywood! How *mar*vellous!' (p. 78). By restoring the original italic, we can now fully appreciate the colloquial register of the writing.

Other changes, now apparent, were to phrases considered in the 1950s to be too American, like 'pretty lavish' and 'stark staring mad', deletions of repetitious phrases (which, it can be argued, Salinger deployed in order to show Holden's obsessiveness), and the substitution of dashes for obscenities like 'Goddam' and 'fuck' – a common publishing practice in the 1950s when laws on obscenity and blasphemy were much stricter than now. Their restoration in 1994 lacks the shock-value now, that they would have had in the 1950s.

Part 2

Summaries

of THE CATCHER IN THE RYE

General summary

The narrator and central character, Holden Caulfield, is a boy of seventeen years of age. The story that he tells takes place over a period of four days from the middle of a Saturday afternoon just a few days prior to the Christmas holidays. However, the events that he recounts are on many levels of time as he recalls several incidents from his past life.

At the opening of the story he tells us that he has been expelled from Pencey Prep. After a row with his roommate, Stradlater, he decides to leave the school before the term ends and takes a train to New York where he rents an hotel room. Most of the book's action takes place in the city. Holden visits a bar and a nightclub. He meets many characters whom he dislikes and gets involved with a young prostitute who cheats him of his money. Having checked out of the hotel he makes a date with an old friend and passes the intervening time wandering around the city. He becomes increasingly disgusted with the quality of most people's social life and manners and asks Sally Hayes to run away with him. When she refuses he continues his aimless rambling around New York and makes yet another date which also proved to be a failure.

Eventually Holden goes home, and, unknown to his parents, has a long conversation with his young sister, Phoebe. Phoebe fails to persuade him to stay and he leaves to resume his pointless tour of the city. When his sister eventually joins him and proposes that they should run away together he becomes angry. After taking her on a visit to the zoo he goes home. In the final chapter Holden tells us that he is in a psychiatric institution on the West coast and is uncertain about his future plans. He ends by expressing his regret at having composed this confessional narrative.

Detailed summaries

Chapter 1: Holden introduces himself to the reader

Holden gives a few very brief details about his family and tells of his expulsion from Pencey, an exclusive private school for young boys. The story as told by Holden begins on a Saturday afternoon shortly before the start of the Christmas school holiday and the main events in the novel take place over a period of four days.

NOTES AND GLOSSARY:

In the opening chapter we are given some essential background information about the narrator and central character, Holden Caulfield. However Holden emphasises that his story is going to be very different from traditional autobiographies such as *David Copperfield* (1849–50) by the English novelist Charles Dickens (1812–70). He says that he will not go into detail about his family and home background because he believes it would be tedious for the reader and really annoy his parents if he revealed details of their family life. This attitude does much to form the reader's view of the boy as an intelligent, precocious and troubled adolescent. Furthermore, his manner of recalling events in a seemingly haphazard way reveals that Salinger is more concerned with portraying the workings of a teenager's mind than with telling a traditional kind of story in which all the details are clearly and logically outlined.

The story dispenses with strict chronology and, instead, follows the movements of Holden's chance reminiscences and arbitrary observations. Thus the use of the 'flashback' technique is the most significant narrative device in the book as it allows us to see the way in which Holden's disorganised thoughts and memories reveal his character and present plight.

In this chapter Holden's most striking characteristic, his sincerity, becomes apparent. He constantly attempts to see people and things as they really are and is contemptuous of everything that is false and dishonest. Indeed, 'phony', which means 'insincere' or 'hypocritical', is the key term in his evaluation of his experience. For example, he refers to Thurmer, Pencey's headmaster, as a 'phony slob' and is scornful towards his brother, D.B., who has squandered his true talent in order to make a lot of money writing scripts for Hollywood films.

In this opening episode of the novel we encounter Holden's idiosyncratic manner of speech which characterises him as a modern, intelligent teenager. The following are the most common and obvious of his particular usages:

(1) A consistent use of slang and colloquial expressions such as 'lousy', 'crap', 'and all', 'crumby', 'it killed me', 'strictly for the birds'.
(2) The use of direct address to the reader.
(3) The employment of nouns as adjectives as in the phrase, 'David Copperfield kind of crap'.
(4) Persistent use of wild exaggeration.

(For a fuller discussion of Holden's speech, see the section 'Language', in Part 3, p. 39.)

lousy: miserable

and all: details like that. Holden uses this expression very frequently

David Copperfield: the main character in Charles Dickens's autobiographical novel of the same name
crap: nonsense
pretty: very
touchy: sensitive
madman stuff: strange experiences
crumby: awful
buck: a dollar
dough: money
regular: ordinary
it killed me: it impressed me greatly
being a prostitute: selling his talents for money
hot-shot guy: impressive man
strictly for the birds: confidentially
the hell up: very high up
too hot: too clearly
faggy: pathetically few
falsies: supports used by some females to make their breasts appear larger than they actually are
horse manure: stupid talk
phony slob: insincere person
goddam: a colloquial swearword often used by Holden
Very big deal: used ironically to mean the opposite
grippe: influenza
flunking: failing
got the ax: expelled
cold as . . .: a colloquial expression meaning very cold
dorm: dormitory, sleeping area
t.b.: tuberculosis
closet: cupboard
crew cut: style of haircut in which the hair is cut very short and trained to grow straight up

Chapter 2: Holden says goodbye to Mr Spencer

Holden pays a farewell visit to an old teacher, Mr Spencer. Spencer gives the boy a lecture on his lack of responsibility and embarrasses Holden by reading passages from his examination script. Holden feels sorry for the old man but is glad to depart after his visit.

NOTES AND GLOSSARY:

The interview with Mr Spencer gives the reader a good insight into Holden's character. His reaction to the old man is a mixture of admiration, sympathy and contempt. He feels sorry for Spencer's senility and, at the same time, he is disgusted by the effects of age on the human body. This mixture of emotions is typical of Holden throughout the novel. His account of the visit shows both his intelligence and his immaturity. He is able to recall a situation in vivid detail and makes several discerning observations. At the same time his feelings are confused and he is unable to concentrate fully on the immediate issue. His mind has a tendency to wander off, as when he wonders about the ducks in Central Park. He also reveals his growing preoccupation with 'phonies' when he talks of his days at Elkton Hills and remembers its headmaster, Mr Hass, whom he describes as the biggest hypocrite he ever met.

a bang: fun, enjoyment
half-assed: mild
Navajo: American Indian tribe
Yellowstone Park: large wildlife park in Wyoming
***Atlantic Monthly*:** American literary journal
crazy about: fond of
ratty: worn
didn't know his ass . . .: didn't know anything
hit the ceiling: got angry
hot-shots: a contemptuous term for clever people who exploit others
carry: pass
Beowulf: oldest English epic poem, probably composed in the early part of the eighth century
Lord Randal: a character in an eighteenth-century Scottish ballad
flunked: failed
chiffonier: a kind of chest of drawers
turd: excreta
shot the bull: put on an act
wasn't up his alley: wasn't of any interest to him
hasn't really hit me: I haven't fully realised

Chapter 3: Holden encounters Robert Ackley

Holden returns to his room in the Ossenburger Memorial Hall and gives a brief, humorous description of Mr Ossenburger whom he calls a 'big phony bastard'. He tells of his favourite literature and recalls an encounter with Robert Ackley, the boy in the neighbouring room.

NOTES AND GLOSSARY:

Holden's confession that he is an incorrigible liar points to the confusion in his adolescent personality. This remark is a clue to his tendency towards self-deception which continues throughout the story. His attitude to writers is symptomatic of his habit of rigorously dividing people into those he loves and those he detests. The subsequent account of Ackley's visit is a fine example of Holden's ability to describe such encounters in lively and amusing detail. However, his relationship with the elder boy reveals once more Holden's acutely sensitive nature. As in the episode with Mr Spencer, Holden is both disgusted by and sympathetic towards his unattractive visitor. Ackley is physically grotesque, yet Holden responds instinctively to his isolation in spite of the fact that his remarks to Ackley are full of schoolboy sarcasm and contempt.

corny: old fashioned
regular guy: a good fellow
stiffs: corpses
swell: good
sore: annoyed
foils: swords
Isak Dinesen: the pseudonym used by the Danish author, Baroness Karen Blixen (1895–1961), who lived for some years on a farm in Kenya
Ring Lardner: Lardner (1885–1933) was an American journalist and story writer
***The Return of the Native*:** (1878), a novel by the English novelist and poet, Thomas Hardy (1840–1928)
knock me out: excite me
***Of Human Bondage*:** a novel by the English writer, Somerset Maugham (1874–1965), published in 1915
Eustacia Vye: a character in Hardy's novel, *The Return of the Native*
roomed: lived
a goner: one who is caught
horsing around: fooling
nope: no
date: girlfriend
handy: at hand
sonuvabitch: son of a bitch, a common American term of abuse
hound's tooth jacket: check-patterned woollen jacket

Chapter 4: Holden holds a long conversation with Stradlater

Holden accompanies Stradlater to the bathroom and talks to him while Stradlater prepares to go on a date with Jane Gallagher, a girl whom Holden knows and likes. Stradlater asks Holden to write a composition for him. When Stradlater departs Ackley returns.

NOTES AND GLOSSARY:

This episode shows Salinger's ability to write lively and convincing adolescent dialogue. Holden's boredom and growing frustration cause him to chatter idly to Stradlater who is totally engrossed in his toilet. Holden's comments upon his friend's vanity are very amusing and reveal one of his most characteristic devices, wild exaggeration. He remarks on the length of time it takes Stradlater to get ready and says that all that time before the mirror is typical of his vanity. Holden's concern about Jane Gallagher's safety in the company of his roommate is wholly in keeping with his constant concern for the weak and vulnerable.

can:	lavatory
chewed the rag:	talked
slob:	uncouth person
Year Book:	the school's annual record of events
up the creek:	in trouble
buddy:	friend
sink:	score points
Oxford:	Oxford University, England
***Ziegfeld Follies*:**	a film of showgirl entravaganza
Sharp:	stylish
B.M. and Shipley:	Bryn Mawr and Shipley are two American women's colleges
checkers:	the board game draughts
caddy:	to carry a golfer's clubs
booze hound:	heavy drinker
rile:	annoy

Chapter 5: Holden goes to the cinema and writes the composition

Holden, Mal Brossard and Ackley go into the town. They plan to see a film but, as Ackley and Brossard have already seen the film, they return to Pencey. Holden passes the evening by writing a composition for Stradlater on the subject of his dead brother's baseball glove.

NOTES AND GLOSSARY:

This episode dramatises the boredom of life at Pencey for boys on the threshold of manhood. Holden's reluctance to fling the snowball at the car is typical of his almost hyper-sensitivity to all that is beautiful and fragile. His account of his violent reaction to Allie's early death tells us a good deal about his psychological state. He reveals that he spent the night of his brother's death in the garage, and that he expressed his sorrow by breaking all the windows with his fists. Here and throughout the rest of the narrative we realise that Holden's most attractive characteristics, his innate gentleness and sensitivity towards people who are vulnerable, is also his greatest weakness. He is completely incapable of accepting the harsh realities of a life in which 'phonies' often survive and prosper while the innocent often suffer defeat. It is his naïve idealism that has led to his breakdown.

racket: cheat
Brown Betty: a kind of apple pudding
crazy: keen on
fiend: enthusiast
Buick: a large car, now manufactured by a division of General Motors
shooting the crap: exaggerating
outside of: besides
hot: well
halitosis: bad breath

Chapter 6: Stradlater attacks Holden

Stradlater returns from his date and reads the composition. He is dissatisfied with it and an argument follows which results in Stradlater hitting Holden in the face. Holden, all bloody, retreats into Ackley's room.

NOTES AND GLOSSARY:
Holden's concern for Jane Gallagher's safety and Stradlater's annoyance about the composition spark off the angry exchange between the two roommates. The ever growing frustration which leads to this encounter is dramatically conveyed in Holden's account of the incident. The bad-tempered exchange between the two boys is vividly realised in Salinger's skilful handling of dialogue which is one of the most striking aspects of the novel as a whole.

griping: complaining
backasswards: in the wrong way
faculty guy: teacher
Give her the time: have sexual intercourse with her
slam ya one: hit you

Chapter 7: Holden prepares to leave Pencey

Holden proposes sleeping Ely's bed, but Ackley is against this proposal. When Ackley has gone to sleep Holden decides to leave the school and plans to spend a few days in New York before returning to his parents. He packs his bags and leaves Pencey.

NOTES AND GLOSSARY:
Holden's growing isolation is evident in this chapter. He remarks several times on his sense of loneliness which is brought about by Ackley's

complete lack of sympathy for his plight. His decision to leave the school marks the end of an episode in his life.

Wuddaya: what do you
Canasta: a card game
killed me: annoyed me
don'tcha: don't you
stark staring: very
Abraham Lincoln: Lincoln (1809–65) was the sixteenth president of the United States. His honesty became legendary
way the hell up: upright
You're aces: you are a good person
swell: good
shot: on edge
Gladstones: light travelling bags
Spaulding's: a sports shop
pretty loaded: fairly rich
a wad: a large sum of money in notes
she doesn't have . . .: she's not wholly sane

Chapter 8: The train journey to New York

Holden takes the night train to New York and passes the time talking to the mother of one of his former classmates at Pencey, Ernest Morrow.

NOTES AND GLOSSARY:
This encounter with Ernest Morrow's mother affords Holden the opportunity to act in an adult, sophisticated manner. His tendency to tell wildly imaginative lies about himself is also very evident. So, too, is his natural kindness and courtesy to people whom he instinctively likes.

the sack: bed
kill me: amuse me
janitor: caretaker
lousy with rocks: wearing many diamonds
Newark: city just south of New York
a hot one: a big lie
matinee: afternoon theatre performance

Chapter 9: Holden arrives in New York

When he reaches New York Holden considers phoning someone but decides that it is too late in the evening. He takes a room in the Edmont hotel and discovers that it is a low-class establishment. He finally calls Faith Cavendish who refuses to join him for a late drink.

NOTES AND GLOSSARY:

Holden's first evening in New York reveals his basic insecurity in the adult world. His immaturity is evident in his mixed reaction to the sight of the transvestite in the opposite room and to the man and woman who amuse themselves by spitting their drinks over each other's face. This latter event causes Holden to examine his own complex and confused attitudes to sex which ends with the confession that sex is incomprehensible to him. This frankness is one of the boy's most appealing characteristics. It is because he so often admits to his own limitations that his attempts to act in a sophisticated way are both amusing and touching. His attempt to overcome the lack of experience is humorously and subtly exposed in his clumsy phone call to Faith Cavendish.

buzz: phone call
shack up: sleep
wise guy: sarcastic person
tryna: trying to
screwball: madman
highballs: cocktails
lousy with: full of
crumby: perverted
horny: sexy
Princeton: prestigious American university
burlesque stripper: nightclub stripper

Chapter 10: An evening in the hotel's Lavender Room

Holden is unable to sleep and decides to spend the remainder of the evening in the hotel's bar. There he meets three girls on a visit to New York. He dances with each of them but finds their company very dull. When they leave he has to pay the bill for their drinks.

NOTES AND GLOSSARY:

This episode in the bar marks the beginning of the novel's criticism of American society. Holden, in spite of his immaturity, is imaginative and possesses an enquiring mind. The three secretaries, on the other hand, lack these qualities. They are typical of many people in a society whose vision of life has been largely shaped by the false world of the Hollywood film industry.

Holden's conversation with the girls is very satiric. He sarcastically remarks to the silent, blonde girl that she is an interesting conversationalist. When the three have departed he condemns their lack of any sense of adventure or discovery, and remarks that it depresses him greatly to learn that their only interest in a visit to New York was to rise early in the morning for the first performance at Radio City Music Hall. He says he would have bought them lots of drinks had they not mentioned this plan.

Holden's intense love and admiration for his ten-year-old sister, Phoebe, is clearly symptomatic of his alienation from an unsympathetic and uncaring adult world. The little girl is, ironically, the only person to whom he can talk with confidence.

shooting the crap: chatting
wizard: genius
giving her the old eye: giving her suggestive looks
strictly from hunger: starved looking
to give . . . the once over: to have sex with
grools: a made-up word meaning a stupid person
part: parting
Wudga: what did you
toleja: told you
butt: backside
murder: awful
Tom Collinses: a summer cocktail of gin, lime juice and soda water

Chapter 11: Holden thinks about Jane Gallagher

Holden sits in the hotel lobby and thinks about his relationship with Jane Gallagher. He finds the memory of her date with Stradlater depressing, and so he decides to cheer himself up by going to a night club.

NOTES AND GLOSSARY:

This chapter is a digression from the main events in Holden's story. His recollection of his friendship with Jane Gallagher shows, yet again, his sensitivity towards others. However, his almost irrational reaction to the memory of Stradlater's relationship with the girl is characteristic of his own confused emotional state.

Doberman pinscher: fierce breed of dog
stink: fuss
the big freeze: the cold shoulder, a cold response
knocked me out: impressed me
muckle-mouthed: with a large, mobile mouth
Maine: state on east coast, north of New York
Cape Cod: cape south of the Gulf of Maine
LaSalle: make of car
glider: swinging sun chair with awning
get wise with: make a pass at
first base: the first stage
Greenwich Village: bohemian quarter of New York

Chapter 12: A visit to Ernie's nightclub

Holden takes a taxi to a nightclub where he meets a number of unpleasant people, including his brother's former girlfriend and her escort.

NOTES AND GLOSSARY:

Holden's conversation with the cab driver about the ducks in Central Park is amusing and shows his curiosity and concern for things which appear trivial to most people. The events in the nightclub reveal Holden's acute, almost paranoid awareness of the vanity, stupidity and pretentiousness of the majority of people around him. Ernie is a 'phony', the Yale Student is a complete bore and Lillian Simmons, his brother's former girlfriend, is totally insincere. Having been forced to shake hands with Lillian's escort and to exchange the conventional polite comments with him, Holden acknowledges that social occasions always force people into hypocritical exchanges. This is the first obvious reference to what is one of the novel's central themes: the way in which society compromises the individual's freedom.

tossed his cookies: been sick
shoot the bull: chat
***sore*:** annoyed
ain'tcha: aren't you
jam-packed: full of people
jerks: uninteresting people
really stinking it up: playing with vigour
frozen Daiquiris: sophisticated, rum-based drink
dope fiend: drug addict
minimum: the smallest quantity of alcohol which it is compulsory to buy in a nightclub
Joe Yale-looking: typical Yale University student
Tattersall vests: type of waistcoat
Ivy League: the most prestigious American universities
crocked: drunk
knockers: female breasts
pansy: effeminate male

Chapter 13: Holden's encounter with the prostitute

Holden walks back to the hotel from Ernie's. On arrival he is solicited by the elevator operator who offers to get him a prostitute. Holden accepts the offer and goes to his room where he nervously awaits the girl's arrival. When she does come Holden is upset and only wants to talk to her.

NOTES AND GLOSSARY:
The meetings with the elevator operator and the young prostitute show Holden's lack of knowledge of the ways of the world. His naïveté and his attempts to assume an adult pose are both touching and funny. Holden's puzzled reminiscences about girls and the mysteries of sex give us a good insight into his troubled character. His confusion abut the real expectations of girls in sexual encounters as well as the callous behaviour of the prostitute constitute an implied criticism of the mores of American urban society.

gorgeous: used ironically here to imply a long way
swiped: stolen
yellow: cowardly
sock: hit
snotty: nasty
Innarested . . .?: are you interested?
tail: sex
throw: one turn
rake: womaniser
spooky: frightening

Chapter 14: Holden is cheated and abused

The elevator operator and the prostitute come to Holden's room and demand an extra five dollars. The boy refuses to pay but the girl takes the money from his wallet. The pimp bullies Holden and hits him in the stomach before departing. When they leave he imagines taking his revenge but soon grows depressed.

NOTES AND GLOSSARY:
Here Holden's vulnerability is very apparent in spite of the fact that he shows a lot of courage in his refusal to pay the money. His wish-fulfilling dream of revenge is cut short when he realises that it is modelled on the clichés – the outworn dramatic situations – of Hollywood detective films. He says that films can corrupt you. In this remark Holden is criticising the phony basis of much contemporary urban culture. (See also the encounter with the three girls in Chapter 10).

BB guns: type of guns which don't require a licence
chisel: cheat
roughin': beating
sharp: smart
wutchamacallit: what do you call it
awreddy: already
rubbernecks: loafers

Chapter 15: Holden leaves the hotel

Holden phones Sally Hayes and makes a date with her before checking out of the hotel. He goes to Grand Central Station where he deposits his luggage and has breakfast. During the meal he engages two nuns in conversation and insists that they accept a ten-dollar contribution for some charity, even though he is running short of money.

NOTES AND GLOSSARY:

Holden's spontaneous generosity towards the nuns is wholly in character and his immediate acceptance of them is in keeping with his usual practice of allocating every chance acquaintance to the ranks of the phonies or non-phonies. His long recollection of a former roommate, Dick Slagle, and his embarrassment over his cheap suitcases, is yet another condemnation of the false values inculcated by a society whose scale of worth is based largely on material wealth. He admits that having better quality luggage than your roommate makes sharing with him difficult in spite of its obvious irrelevance to his worth as a person. The reason is that it makes even witty and intelligent people self-conscious.

Holden's immediate liking for the nuns springs from an awareness of their unworldliness. But it is ironic that he can only express his feelings towards them by making a money donation. He concludes by observing that money always causes problems.

Benefits: charity shows
chewed the fat: chatted
Harvard: a prestigious university in Boston, founded in 1636
freshman: first-year student
West Point: United States Military Academy in New York
Broadway: the most famous street in New York
Salvation Army: an international, Christian charitable organisation which is organised along military lines
Grendel: monster in *Beowulf*
Nationals at Forest Hills: Tennis tournaments
blue as hell: very sad

Chapter 16: Holden wanders around the city

Holden has two spare hours before his date with Sally Hayes so he walks to Broadway in search of a particular record for his sister, Phoebe. Having bought the record and the tickets for the show, he goes to Central Park in the hope of meeting Phoebe there. He next walks to the Museum of Natural History, but, having realised that Phoebe certainly won't be inside, he decides not to go in and instead takes a taxi to the Biltmore theatre.

NOTES AND GLOSSARY:

This chapter is typical of Salinger's dramatic methods in the novel as a whole. Nothing of any importance takes place; Holden merely buys a record and theatre tickets, talks to some children, observes a small boy and his parents and walks to the doors of the museum. There are no 'dramatic' incidents. What is of interest and significance takes place inside the mind of the central character. We learn a lot about Holden from his observations and comments upon all the casual phenomena which he sees on his ramble around the city. He is totally preoccupied with the quality of people's lives and with distinguishing between the sincere and the phony in all aspects of American culture. A list of his reactions to some of the things he sees or remembers in this chapter will illustrate the point:

(1) He compares his aunt's selfish way of life with that of the nuns whom he met in the previous chapter.
(2) He admires the sincerity of Estelle Fletcher's rendering of 'Little Shirley Beans' and compares her 'Dixieland and whorehouse' style to the more usual 'cute' and commercial arrangements made of such songs by white singers.
(3) The spontaneity and joy of the little boy's song cheers him up. Holden is attracted to most children because of their innocence. They have not yet been corrupted by the ways of the society in which they live.
(4) The people rushing to get to the cinemas irritate him. Holden regards the movies as a form of mindless entertainment. He says that he gets annoyed by people who go to the cinema because they actually enjoy movies rather than going simply to pass the time.
(5) He regards the show, *I Know My Love*, as a piece of sentimental trash and admits he bought tickets for it only because the insincere Sally would be excited at the prospect of seeing the Lunts. He goes on to remark on the insincerity of the majority of actors and cites the famous English actor, Laurence Olivier, as an example. Holden confesses that he is only comfortable when reading the text of a play and that he fears the potential insincerity of the performance of actors.

As is clear in this chapter, Holden's breakdown was brought about by his hyper-sensitive nature. He takes nothing for granted but analyses even insignificant things against his undefined, if very real, ideals. His love of children, especially his sister, Phoebe, suggests a fear of the adult world. This distaste for life, with all its inevitable imperfections, is implicit in his praise of the static world contained within the wall of the museum.

Holden reflects that the attraction of the museum is that all its exhibits are static and that on each visit the Eskimo and the fish he has caught are in the same position. Indeed the only thing that would have changed would be the observer.

for the hell of it: for fun
knock out: please greatly
Dixieland and whorehouse: a style of 'blues' singing which originated in the American south
hung out: spent her free time
sharp: fashionable
swell: great
mobbed: crowded
Lunts: the actor Alfred Lunt and his actress wife Lynne Fontanne
dry: ironic
big bang: much enjoyment
Ferdinand and Isabella: King and Queen of Spain

Chapter 17: The date with Sally

Holden and Sally visit the theatre and afterwards they go ice skating at Radio City. They have an argument and Sally rushes home in an angry mood.

NOTES AND GLOSSARY:

Holden's behaviour in this chapter is wholly in character. His mixed attitudes to the girls waiting for their dates and to the memory of the boring Harris Macklin, is typical of his confused reactions to many things in the novel. However, his almost violent and unreasonable response to Sally's behaviour is clearly meant by Salinger to be a rejection of all that is worst in American middle-class life and culture. Having expressed his dislike of school he goes on to articulate his contempt for life in New York: the traffic, the noise, the social scene. He even finds such mundane activities as using elevators and getting fitted for pants to be irritating.

In spite of the justness of many of Holden's criticisms of life, there is often an irrationality in his reactions to trivial events and details, a reaction which is barely kept in check by his wit and humour.

bunk: nonsense
jerk: stuffy person
big soul kiss: a passionate kiss
Andover: distinguished college for men
to puke: to vomit
to horn in on: to take part uninvited
blocks: streets
lulus: bad ones
Brooks: prestigious New York tailor's
oodles of: lots of

Chapter 18: Holden telephones some friends

Because he is lonely, Holden tries to contact some of his friends on the telephone before going to the cinema.

NOTES AND GLOSSARY:

There is little of dramatic interest in this chapter. Holden merely makes some phone calls and goes to the cinema. But, as usual, it is his reflections on the life around him that are of significance. His parody-like synopses of the Christmas show and the war film are an adverse criticism of the sentimentality and bad taste of the American public. His reaction to some of the great works of modern American literature is based on his sense of what is truly authentic. Significantly, he is 'crazy about' *The Great Gatsby* as it is one of the most trenchant critiques of the ills of American society.

a malted: a malted milk
Fourth of July: Independence Day
Choate: American college
half gainer: type of dive
Columbia: a university in New York
homey: domestic
furlough: leave
***A Farewell to Arms*:** a novel by Ernest Hemingway (1899–1961), published in 1929
Ring Lardner: Lardner (1885–1933) was an American journalist and writer of satiric short stories about various aspects of American life
***The Great Gatsby*:** a famous novel about American high society by F. Scott Fitzgerald (1896–1940). It was first published in 1925 and portrays the corrupt side of American idealism and the class system in the decades after the 1914–18 world war

Chapter 19: The meeting at the Wicker Bar

Holden meets a former acquaintance, Carl Luce, in the Wicker Bar and their conversation is mainly about sex.

NOTES AND GLOSSARY:

The meeting with Carl Luce gives the reader a deeper insight into Holden's character. The fact that he doesn't really like Luce emphasises the extent of his loneliness and his need for some sympathetic human contact. Holden's attempt to discuss the mysteries of sex points to the immaturity that lies beneath his adult veneer. Much of Holden's trouble comes from the fact that he is more mature mentally than emotionally. In fact he shows an awareness of this during his conversation with Carl Luce.

snowing hell out of: flattering
flits: homosexuals
the Village: Greenwich Village – the bohemian quarter of New York
Nantucket: seaside resort in Massachusetts
tear: run

Chapter 20: A walk in Central Park

Holden is drunk when he leaves the bar. He has nothing to do so he walks through Central Park. After a short time he decides to go home and talk to Phoebe.

NOTES AND GLOSSARY:
This episode reveals the full extent of Holden's loneliness as his mind turns to thoughts of death and to memories of his late brother, Allie.

hat-check room: cloakroom
spookier: more ghostly

Chapter 21: Holden talks to Phoebe

Holden manages to get into his parents' flat without being recognised. He reads through some of Phoebe's notebooks before waking her. At first she is pleased and excited to see him, but when she realises that he has been expelled from school she loses her temper.

NOTES AND GLOSSARY:
Holden's love for his young sister and for children in general is very obvious in this chapter. He regards childhood as a state of perfection in which there are no 'phonies'. Looking at the sleeping child, he observes that adults look awful when they are asleep, unlike children who look sweet even when they drool on their pillows.

break: stroke of luck
slob: untidy person
Benedict Arnold: a general in the War of Independence and a traitor
Lister Foundation: charitable foundation for scientific research
grippy: ill
C'*mon*: come on
all out: exhausted

Chapter 22: Holden confides in Phoebe

Phoebe is very annoyed with her brother and asks him if there is *anyone* he likes or *anything* he would like to be. He replies by explaining why he hated Pencey and remembers the suicide of James Castle. He also thinks about the two nuns whom he met at Grand Central Station. He confesses that he would like to be the protector of small children playing in a big field of rye. He admits that it is a silly desire, but insists that it is what he would really like to do.

NOTES AND GLOSSARY:

Phoebe is much more realistic than her brother in spite of her age. The things that Holden dislikes have one fact in common. They are all manifestations of the absence of love and compassion in human life. His inability to adjust to life's inevitable shortcomings lies at the heart of his despair and impending breakdown. His dream of being the catcher in the rye is, he realises, a fantasy which is indicative of his great desire to make a better world. This fantasy is, of course, totally in keeping with his consistent attitude to children throughout the novel. His dream of saving the children from falling over the cliff is really a desire to preserve their childhood state and to stop their 'fall' into adulthood and inevitable wickedness.

ostracizing: rejecting
snotty: nasty, superior, stuck-up
bull session: fooling around
fraternity: brotherhood, group
yellow: cowardly
to be incognito: not recognisable, not seen
Veterans' Day: Old boys' reunion day
1776: the date of the beginning of the War of Independence
cockeyed: crooked
N.Y.U.: New York University

Chapter 23: Holden escapes discovery by his parents

Holden phones a former teacher, Mr Antolini, who offers to give him a bed for the night. His parents return before he leaves and he hides in the closet. Phoebe covers up for him and lends him her Christmas money before he departs.

NOTES AND GLOSSARY:

This scene skilfully evokes the love between Holden and his young sister without any trace of sentimentality. It also serves to emphasise his isolation from his parents and contemporaries.

snappy:	brief
Yogi guys:	people who practise Yoga
numbers:	tunes

Chapter 24: Holden goes to the Antolini apartment

Mr Antolini gives Holden some 'good' advice and then makes up a bed for him on the couch. Holden is exhausted and goes to sleep immediately. However, he later wakes up to find Antolini stroking his hair. He is frightened and leaves the apartment in a great hurry.

NOTES AND GLOSSARY:

Antolini's analysis of Holden's shortcomings is an accurate and perceptive one in spite of his increasing drunkenness. However, it is too theoretical and academic to be of any help or comfort to the exhausted boy. Holden obviously needs love and sympathy rather than moral advice. His suspicion that his former teacher is making a homosexual advance destroys his image of him.

witty:	clever
oiled up:	drunk
ace:	first class
driving at:	talking about
Wilhelm Stekel:	misspelling of Steckel, a contemporary of Jung and Freud in the field of psycho-analysis
hot:	in the mood
trusty:	large

Chapter 25: Holden spends the afternoon with Phoebe

It is now early on Monday morning and Holden returns to Grand Central Station. He is unable to sleep in the waiting room and goes for a walk. He begins to feel ill and feverish. He then decides to go west and work, pretending to be deaf and dumb so as to avoid all contact with people. He next goes to Phoebe's school and leaves a note asking her to meet him at the museum. She arrives late carrying one of his old suitcases and explains that she plans to run away with him. Holden becomes angry with her. When he goes to the zoo she follows him at a distance and there they make up their quarrel. Phoebe rides on the carousel and Holden feels unusually happy. He promises to return home with her.

NOTES AND GLOSSARY:

This chapter reveals the imminent approach of Holden's nervous breakdown. His resolve to escape from society into the outback ends in a tacit admission of defeat. His constant awareness of the world's shortcomings proves his final undoing. He hasn't been able to make the kind of adjustment to life's imperfections that is necessary in order to live a 'normal' life.

stark staring mad: very excited
bum a ride: hitch a lift
recess: free time
taken a leak: gone to the lavatory
all cockeyed: wrong
shot the breeze: chatted
brudda: brother
awreddy: already
beat it: ran off
a yella streak: cowardly
hit the road: started the journey
carrousel: roundabout or merry-go-round
bawling: crying

Chapter 26: Holden ends his story

Holden tells the reader that this account of his mental illness has been written since his arrival in some clinic where he has been undergoing psychoanalysis. He says that he is sorry that he told so much as it has made him miss all the people he wrote about, even Stradlater, Ackley and Maurice, the elevator attendant.

NOTES AND GLOSSARY:

This short final chapter serves four obvious purposes:

(1) It puts the narrative as a whole into perspective by explaining the reason for its composition.
(2) It lends conviction to the book's conversational tone and apparently rambling narrative form.
(3) It concludes the work in a satisfactory way.
(4) It suggests that Holden's programme of psychoanalysis has been largely unsuccessful. His attitudes and hopes for the future as expressed here hint that he will continue to find American life as uncongenial as in the past.

Part 3

Commentary

The Catcher in the Rye as a literary landmark

The Catcher in the Rye was published on 16 July 1951 by Little, Brown of Boston. Salinger had earlier offered the novel to Robert Giroux, an editor at the publisher Harcourt, Brace and both men shook hands on their agreement to publish it. A year later Salinger sent the manuscript of *The Catcher in the Rye* to Giroux who regarded himself lucky to be the editor of such a remarkable book. However, Giroux's boss, Eugene Reynal, was less enthusiastic and his suggested changes and revisions led to the author taking back his manuscript.

Salinger's uneasiness about publishers was probably deepened by Little, Brown's pre-publication publicity campaign. He wanted no publicity and even demanded that his photograph be removed from the back cover. Eventually he consented to its inclusion but, subsequently, had it removed from all editions. All copies of *The Catcher in the Rye* currently on sale throughout the world are remarkable for their lack of photographs and biographical information about the writer.

The British edition of the novel appeared in August 1951. Salinger seems to have held Hamish Hamilton in high regard. However, the trust between Salinger and Hamilton came to an end over what appears to have been a misunderstanding on the writer's part about aspects of the paperback edition of *For Esmé – With Love and Squalor, and Other Stories* (1953). Following this episode Salinger supervised the publication of his works worldwide; his contracts gave him powers to control biographical details, photographic reproductions and quotations from reviews. He appears to have been scrupulous in the exercise of these powers.

The Catcher in the Rye received mixed critical receptions in the USA and in Britain. Journals like *The Christian Science Monitor* and *Catholic World* attacked it for its 'formidably excessive use of amateur swearing and coarse language'. The reviewer for the *New York Herald Tribune* also expressed misgivings about the novel's language saying that it 'repeats and repeats, like an incantation'. In Britain, the writer in the *Times Literary Supplement* found Holden 'very touching' but added that 'the endless stream of blasphemy and obscenity in which he talks, credible as it is, palls after the first chapter'. *Punch* (London) judged the book to be over 'sentimental' and added, condescendingly, that this 'may be merely a reaction of a corrupt European who prefers a soft surface and a hard core'.

Perhaps the most disenchanted review of all appeared in *Commentary* in January 1952. In it William Poster attacked the creator behind the creation. He wrote: 'The ennui, heartburn, and weary revulsions of *The Catcher in the Rye* are the inevitable actions, not of an adolescent, however disenchanted, but of a well paid satirist with a highly developed technique, no point of view, and no target to aim at but himself.'

On the other hand, many reviewers were very impressed and Salinger's novel was the Book-of-the-Month Club's selection for July 1951. The Club's Clifton Fadiman wrote: 'That rare miracle of fiction has again come to pass: a human being has been created out of ink and paper and the imagination.' On the day the novel was published the *New York Times* called it 'an unusually brilliant first novel'. The *Chicago Tribune* said that it was 'engaging and believable' and remarked that it was 'full of right observation and sharp insight'. *The Catcher in the Rye* received similar praise in other journals.

In spite of the many reviews that attempted to add Salinger's novel to the canon of American literature, the moral revulsion articulated by *The Christian Science Monitor* and the *Catholic World* was reflected in widespread formal censorship. The book's alleged 'immorality and perversion' were accepted by a large number of school boards and public library committees as cause to ban it from their classrooms and shelves. There have been numerous accounts of teachers who were either suspended or fired from their jobs for including the story of Holden Caulfield on the curriculum. The work that *Time* magazine, in its account of the dismissal of a teacher in 1960 in Tulsa, Oklahoma, referred to as 'the most avidly admired novel on modern American campuses' continues to be the cause of moral stricture. There are still libraries that ban this book from their shelves and schools that will not permit their pupils to study it.

In Britain and in Europe such moral outrage, when it was expressed, was more muted. In Britain, too, sales were more modest than they had been in the United States where it became an instant bestseller. By 1970 it had been translated into over thirty languages, and worldwide it has sold more than 60 million copies.

When the initial celebrity and notoriety passed, Salinger confessed that he felt relieved that the fuss had died down and that he would no longer have to look at his face in every bookstore. But by the late 1950s and the early 1960s *The Catcher in the Rye* had acquired cult status amongst American college students. It had also become a text for academic scrutiny and was proclaimed an American classic by some. Others, like George Steiner writing in *The Nation* in 1959, objected to the inflated reputation of the author and to 'The Salinger Industry' in general. The intense critical interest of those years has died down, though there continues to be published a number of articles each year and the occasional scholarly book. Sales of *The Catcher in the Rye* continue to be the envy of most writers;

it is calculated that 250,000 copies are sold each year throughout the world. Salinger has published no fiction since 1966; he remains silent and reclusive and, consequently, is of more interest to many readers than his fictional characters.

Contemporary cultural and literary context

In the mid-1950s *The Catcher in the Rye* became the 'in' book on college campuses throughout the United States. In Salinger's five-year-old novel the so-called teenage revolution had found its images of disaffection.

The 'youthquake' of the late 1950s was a result of the 'babyboom' of the immediate postwar years (see *The Catcher in the Rye* and American society p. 8). Market forces were quick to convert the cult of 'outsiderism' of middle-class youth into a cultural industry as exemplified in the film *Rebel Without a Cause* (1955) in which the hoodlums, for the first time, were portrayed as coming from respectable, middle-class families. The young star of that film, James Dean, with his sullen, good looks became a potent icon of youthful alienation, a status that was intensified by his early death in the same year as *Rebel* was released. The huge sales of *The Catcher in the Rye* which took off at about this time are explicable by the fact that it seemed to articulate vague discontentments felt by college students of the day; it continued with the same potency in the 1960s for the generation whose lives were dominated by the war in Vietnam. In spite of its appeal for these later periods, *The Catcher in the Rye* is very much a product of the 1940s. It was conceived during the last years of the Second World War and was published in the middle of the Korean war.

The most apparent period hallmark is the way that the culture of Hollywood is felt in the novel; Holden professes contempt for the movies but has clearly seen many and been influenced by them. Not only does he act out the stylised role of the dying gangster (Chapter 14) but much of his posture and behaviour mimics such screen heroes as Humphrey Bogart: he smokes continuously and has the world-weary air of characters like Rick in *Casablanca* (1943). Holden, too, tells his tale with something of the wise-cracking contempt and tight-lipped cynicism of the narrators of the novels of Dashiell Hammett (1894–1961) and Raymond Chandler (1889–1959). The New York that Holden experiences has occasionally the look and the feel of the underworlds depicted in such films as the adaptations of Hammett's *The Maltese Falcon* (1941) and Chandler's *Farewell My Lovely* (1944) and *The Big Sleep* (1946). This is particularly so in the episode in Ernie's nightclub (Chapter 12) and Holden's experiences with the prostitute and her pimp (Chapters 13 and 14).

But the affinity of the city in the novel to the world of celluloid gangsters is not only a matter of specific similarities; it is also a matter of a more general atmosphere which has become associated with those culturally empty years after the war. Holden's own awareness of the extent to which the movies have conditioned his ways of seeing the world occasions his frustrated cursing of movies. It is significant that he views written fictions and Hollywood fictions as competing narratives within the cultural hierarchy. He imagines his brother, D.B., a movie scriptwriter and novelist *manqué*, paying a visit to the imaginary cabin near the woods. Holden says that he will not permit his brother to write movies, only stories. It is obvious that Holden has seen a large number of films and that he is trying to exorcise their pervasive and baleful influence from his consciousness.

One of the most potent images in *The Catcher in the Rye* is when Holden wishes himself on top of the atomic bomb which seems to prefigure the final scene from Stanley Kubrick's *Dr Strangelove* (1963). Indeed, it is possible to argue that Salinger's novel, though rooted in the 1940s, belongs spiritually to the anti-war, anti-regimentation culture that dominated much American art in the Vietnam war years. The author who attended Valley Forge Military Academy and later served in the army during the Second World War, created in Holden Caulfield a hero whose dislike of regimentation and distrust of authority gave America one of its models of dissent against the ideologies that lay behind US military activities in Asia in the postwar years. To this extent it has something in common with such works of protest and dissent as Joseph Heller's *Catch 22* (1961) and the movie, *M.A.S.H.* (1970).

Holden's status as a symbol of individualism for American youth was largely confined to the middle and upper income groups with backgrounds broadly similar to his own. His is a very specific social world with its own traditions, codes and practices. The Caulfields, though only vaguely portrayed as a unit, are recognisably a financially well-off, New York nuclear family. Pencey is a kind of single-sex boarding school that, from the nineteenth century, educated and socialised young males of the business and professional classes. Such schools were the transmitters of ideals and values of an élite in American life. Holden's contempt for much that he is taught at the school was, for many of his readers, interpreted as a rejection of the complacency and limitations of all that such institutions stood for. His central objection to Pencey is that its spirit of communal care and solidarity is really a mask that disguises its propagation of the selfish, competitive ethos of American life with its power élites and exclusive clubs.

For many readers Holden Caulfield was received as the archetypal, youthful outsider who sustains a commentary on the shortcomings of his society. However, a few saw in him the misfit rather than the true outsider due to the fact that he is unmistakably a product of the world he seeks to shun; he is in fact a young man who reveals the post-industrial culture of North America, characterised by the growing influence of the mass media, the lessening of parental authority and the increasing dominance of peer groups with time on their hands and money in their pockets. In Britain, teenage readers of *The Catcher in the Rye* were as likely to have been impressed by a schoolboy with such spending power, sophistication and mobility as they were by the nature of his protest. In America, too, this was a novel that spoke eloquently to a clearly defined segment of society, most of whom purchased it in campus bookstores.

The hero of Kingsley Amis's novel, *Lucky Jim* (1953), is often cited as Holden Caulfield's English counterpart. But the identification of the two characters only emphasis the enormous differences between their worlds. Holden is responding to a complex adult society in which innocence and idealism cannot survive. Jim Dixon, although a junior lecturer in History at a provincial university, is that eternal English type, the mocking school boy who finds the world of grown-ups silly and oppressive. Unlike Holden, Jim can always escape into the juvenile world of mimicry, mockery and make-believe. Amis's novel is a mildly satiric fairytale; Salinger's is a lament for the inevitable loss of innocence and to that extent is a very American book.

Historical background in literature

On its publication one reviewer referred to *The Catcher in the Rye* as a modern picaresque novel in the tradition of *Huckleberry Finn* (1884). This identification of Salinger's 'study of reluctant pubescence' in an urban setting with Mark Twain's classic tale has become a commonplace of the criticism of the later story.

Huckleberry Finn tells of a fourteen-year-old boy's attempt to escape from the well-meaning ladies who adopt him and try to 'sivilize' him. Huck's impulse is 'to light out for the territory' and so avoid all the constraints upon his freedom. The boy's adventure element of the story is the narrative device upon which Twain constructed a complex analysis of the shortcomings of the so-called 'civilisation' of the American South in the 1840s. Much American writing from the nineteenth century to the present day has been preoccupied by such figures as Huck Finn; the outsider who needs to escape society and tradition in order to realise his true, inner self. The most obvious constriction upon such characters is towns or cities; urban life is always viewed as an existence that is alien to man's true, inner nature. Conversely, it is what Huck Finn refers to as 'the territory', untamed nature, that is conceived as the realm in which a person can grow and prosper.

The individualist and anti-urban strain in American art to which *The Catcher in the Rye* belongs dates back to the early nineteenth century when the old frontier ways of life gave way to the rapid growth of Boston, Philadelphia, New York, San Francisco and other cities. As a consequence, much of the fiction from this period onwards is concerned with the hero's struggles to retain his integrity as the march of civilisation threatens the wilderness and its natural culture. Such preoccupations are found in the *Leatherstocking* novels of James Fenimore Cooper (1789–1851). This frontier myth-making in novels by Cooper such as *The Pioneers* (1823) and *The Prairie* (1827) was popularised and often debased in hundreds of 'dime' novels from about 1860 to the 1920s and later. The fashion for these stories was, to some extent, taken over by the Hollywood movie industry and the figure of the plainsman, such as Cooper's Natty Bumpoo (Hawkeye), and the cowboy hero of Owen Wister's *The Virginian* (1902) became the white-hatted, lone hero of hundreds of motion pictures.

The view of the city as being destructive of man's inner freedom is a recurring theme in modern American literature. The power of the big city to crush the individual's sense of identity is articulated in, for example, Carl Sandburg's 'Chicago' (1916). In this poem the city is evoked as though it had a life of its own, independent and careless of the human beings who live in it:

> Fierce as a dog with tongue lapping for action, cunning as a savage pitted against the wilderness,
> Bearheaded,
> Shoveling,
> Wrecking,
> Planning
> Building, breaking, rebuilding,
> . . .

In his novel, *The Victim* (1947), Saul Bellow describes the central character's experience of crossing to New York's Staten Island:

> . . . the towers on the shore rose up in huge blocks, scorched, smoky gray . . . The notion brushed Leventhal's mind that the light over them and over the water was akin to the yellow revealed in the eye of a wild animal, say a lion, something inhuman that didn't care about anything human . . .

Although Holden Caulfield's New York does not have quite the nightmarish quality of Bellow's description, it is the 'madhouse' from which Salinger's young hero feels he must escape. But in the middle of the twentieth century there is no possibility of a raft on a river as a getaway; Holden's America is far removed in terms of time and space from that of Huck Finn.

Narrative structure

On the surface the narrative sequence of *The Catcher in the Rye* is fairly straightforward. Four days of Holden's experiences are presented chronologically:

(1) Chapters 1–7 relate the events at Pencey school prior to Holden's early departure.
(2) Chapters 8–25 take place in New York City.
(3) Chapter 26, the short epilogue to the novel, reveals that Holden is in a psychiatric clinic. We learn that it is here that he composed this account of his experiences.

The narrative, however, is not strictly chronological. Although Holden sets out to tell what happened over a very short period, he constantly digresses and recounts many and varied episodes from his past life. Therefore, instead of learning about a single episode in his life, we get a fairly comprehensive and full account of his past history. In this respect Salinger employed one of the commonest techniques of twentieth-century fiction. This was the 'flashback', a method of narration whereby the narrator's story is apparently dictated by his random stream of associations and memories. One fact or detail brings another similar or associated incident to mind so that the teller tends to digress from the main point of his story such as we all do in our everyday conversations. In the works of novelists such as James Joyce (1882–1941) or William Faulkner (1897–1962), the digressions are highly organised and controlled and merely give the impression of natural randomness. Their narratives only seem more spontaneous and realistic than those of earlier writers who followed a more obvious and rigid time scale. The same can be said of *The Catcher in the Rye*. Salinger's narrative is very consciously controlled and shaped. He successfully attempts to make the reader believe that Holden's story has all the looseness of organisation that we would expect from a seventeen-year-old boy's story of his adventures over a period of a few days. For instance, Holden's opening words are a self-conscious attempt by the author to imply that his book is not like the great classic autobiographical novels of the nineteenth century. He says that he will not tell the reader all the usual details of birth, parents and childhood such as one used to get in novels like *David Copperfield*; he just does not feel like it (Chapter 1). The casual, slangy tone of the speaker and his dismissal of the conventional autobiographical formula is effective in creating the illusion of a real boy about to give an account of his experience without any conscious organisation. The reader feels that he)s about to hear the facts with all inessential details cast aside. However, on reflection, we realise that Salinger's narrative method is in no sense spontaneous or shapeless. By the time we have finished the story we have received a very full impression of all those factors, including his parents, that have made Holden the person he is.

The novel's plot is, of course, dictated by the kind of narrative method that Salinger used. Events occur in a seemingly arbitrary way as Holden wanders around New York, attempting to ease his 'lonesomeness'. The episodic nature of these chapters shows the author employing one of the oldest of all dramatic narrative devices, the 'picaresque'. The 'picaresque' tale developed in sixteenth-century Spain and the typical story had for its subject the escapades of merry rogues who lived by their wits (*picaro* is the Spanish for rogue). As in Salinger's novel, the plots of these tales were no more than the sum of random adventures experienced by the central characters. Such a loose dramatic structure was well suited to Salinger's purpose in writing *The Catcher in the Rye*. It allowed him to introduce a wide variety of characters into the story. He could let Holden come into contact with various people without sacrificing the story's air of realism as all such meetings are possible on a three-day ramble in a large city. Moreover, this fitted his wider intentions. Salinger wanted to create an impression of the impersonality and callousness of life in a place like New York for an innocent such as Holden Caulfield and this freedom to allow the boy to encounter a cross-section of characters was fundamental to his aim.

The digressive nature of the story is, too, in keeping with the character of Holden himself. He has a liking for digression as have most garrulous people. However, the character who is speaking in the present to the reader/listener from a clinic near Hollywood is dealing with memories at two levels: the recent past that led to his present situation and an earlier past that preceded his few days in New York during which he engages the recollections of, for example, his brother Allie and Jane Gallagher as well as experiences of incidents and places.

It is these three time levels represented in the narrative that embody the complexity of Holden, and it is this temporal complexity that makes it so difficult to decide how much Holden has changed throughout the novel.

Language

The fact that Holden tells his own story in his own words was a large part of the novel's popularity with its first readers. Young people responded to an idiom that appeared similar to their own way of thinking and talking. Many adult readers were offended by the use of vulgar or obscene words as well as occasional blasphemous phrases. It was in part such usages that led to the novel being banned from many public libraries and from school reading lists (see p. 33), a ban that continues in some parts of America to the present day. Although the expletives give the story a sense of freshness of utterance, there are moments when they become tiresome with repetition. It was probably for this reason that the English publisher Hamish Hamilton made a number of deletions from the British edition of the novel and not from considerations of verbal propriety. Indeed, this edition of *The Catcher in the Rye* is, in some respects, more fluent for the alterations to the text (see A note on the text, p. 11).

But Salinger's linguistic invention was not simply a matter of inserting a few 'risky' words into the narrator's mouth. In his creation of Holden he sustained a recognisable and convincing teenage way of speaking in terms of diction, syntax and inflections. The written document that is here represented as a spoken narrative is peculiar, if not exclusive, to the American literary tradition. John Updike, for example, has described Holden's narrative as being, like Philip Roth's Portnoy (*Portnoy's Complaint*, 1969), in the long line 'of the New York voice on the couch, the smart kid's lament'. It was, however, an innocent kid, Mark Twain's *Huckleberry Finn*, who firmly established American colloquial speech as a natural and flexible mode for complex fictional narration as long ago as 1884. Like Holden, Twain's character tells of his adventures in his own words which are free of the grammatical constraints of 'standard' English. The effect is not only a heightened sense of the reality of the tale but an awareness of the pleasure inherent in the language itself with its regional idioms, tones and colours.

Holden Caulfield is a compulsive talker in spite of his early warning that he is not going to tell us his complete life story. There are moments in the story when his talk is calculated to relish the pleasures of his own voice rather than to communicate any particular information. One those occasions when he is accused of talking too much or too loudly we sometimes sense that he is enjoying the rhythms and cadences of the utterances themselves. Sometimes the flow and urgency of his talk is caused by self-consciousness or nervousness, as in his encounter with the prostitute (Chapter 13), or to fill an uncomfortable silence. Holden needs to and loves to talk; a listener, any listener, is essential to his wellbeing.

Because of his vulnerability in the adult world that he is trying to negotiate, Holden uses language in a number of complex ways either to interpret his society or to ward off its incomprehensible or unpalatable complexities and ambiguities. At the most obvious, the 'tough guy' idiom of the 1930s and 1940s gangster novels and movies which he sometimes adopts is a means of concealing his vulnerability behind a linguistic toughness. On the other hand, such moments as his description of the Eskimo in the museum (Chapter 16) is, in its directness and simplicity, perfectly evocative of his sensitive inner nature.

In his creation of Holden he succeeded in sustaining a recognisable and convincing teenage way of speaking in terms of diction, syntax and speech inflexions. Furthermore, he gave to Holden's speech a personal, idiosyncratic flavour so that it is a recognisably individual voice and not a mere reproduction of the average teenager's parlance.

There are two very obvious usages continually employed by Holden which are idiosyncratic and, at the same time, sufficiently typical of teenage speech for them to seem representative. These are:

(1) The ending of a sentence with the dangling phrase, 'and all'.
(2) The use of the emphatic, 'I really did'.

His employment of these phrases is all-pervasive, and they come to form a part of the reader's perception of Holden's character. His constant use of 'and all', 'or something', 'or anything' serves no useful linguistic function. They merely tend to create the sense of loose thought and expression. Occasionally they imply that there is more to be said about the issue in hand, but that he is not going to pursue the subject.

Another of Holden's most characteristic speech habits arises from his determination to emphasise his sincerity. He often uses phrases that include 'really' and tags them on to the ends of statements as though he were afraid of being called a 'phony'.

Holden's rhetorical use of 'if you want to know the truth' is much like his emphatic reiteration of 'really'. Sometimes, however, it is a confession of frankness and conveys the sense that he is aware that his admission might shock the reader but that he must take the risk in the interest of truthfulness. He varies his emphatic manner only occasionally as when, in Chapter 9, he admits that sex is something that he doesn't understand and swears to God for emphasis.

Most of Holden's vulgar or obscene usages are inoffensive and highly colloquial. He repeats such words as 'goddam' or 'sonuvabitch' without any conscious intention of being profane or of insulting a person's mother. Moreover, it is when he is reporting conversations with his contemporaries at school that the majority of these words occur. This points to the fact that these expressions are an integral part of the language of the sub-culture of American schoolboys. Holden's use of 'hell' is a good example of a word which has lost its original meaning and acquired a new currency in his world. The most common function of 'hell' is its use in sentences such as 'a helluva time' and as the second part of a simile as in 'old as hell', 'pretty as hell', 'cold as hell' and 'hot as hell'. In all but the last example 'hell' has almost lost its real meaning and serves much the same function as the word 'very'.

It is striking that Holden avoids the one word which he himself regards as an obscenity, 'fuck'. On the occasions when he sees the word written on walls he becomes extremely angry lest some child should see it and be corrupted by it (see Chapter 25).

Holden's constant use of American slang is often colourful and amusing. But inevitably it sometimes fails as a vehicle for precise communication. His continual use of 'crap' is a good example. His 'crap' has several connotations besides its usual slang meanings of 'excrement' or 'to defecate'. It can mean 'stupidity' as in 'all that David Copperfield kind of crap'. It may also imply an unfavourable judgement as in 'the show was on the crappy side'. The phrase, 'to shoot the crap' sometimes means 'to lie', but it can also mean 'to chat' to someone.

Like 'crap', 'crazy' is a word which has no fixed meaning for Holden. 'That drives me crazy' means that he greatly dislikes something. Yet, 'to be crazy about' something means the exact opposite. Similarly, 'killed' can express contempt or approval depending on the context.

Some of Holden's usages are mere habits and have no real meanings. For instance, he tends to put 'old' before names: 'old Phoebe', 'old Maurice', 'old Jesus'. Likewise, he often employs 'Boy' as an ejaculation.

In spite of the fact that Holden's vocabulary does tend to become repetitious he occasionally hits upon images which are fresh and striking as when he says his teacher handled his exam script as if it were excrement and in so doing showed the sensitivity of a toilet seat. Such earthy, almost surrealistic similes are characteristic of much American urban communication. Indeed, they are one of the most obvious features of the dialogue in the works of 'serious' novelists such as Saul Bellow and Norman Mailer. In this respect the American novel, since the time of Mark Twain, has clearly remained closer to the living language of the majority of people than has its British counterpart.

Evidence of this fact is apparent throughout *The Catcher in the Rye*. For example, Holden's language often reflects the general American adaptability in matters of speech as in most other facets of life. He often turns nouns into adjectives by the addition of a 'y': 'Christmasy', 'show-offy', 'vomity-looking'. He sometimes makes interesting compound words like 'cheerer-upper' and has a tendency to use nouns as adverbs.

Although Holden's speech is often slangy and imprecise, he is, nevertheless, very self-conscious in his use of language. His need to be as truthful as possible with his readers is reflected in the many repetitions and small qualifications that punctuate much of his narrative. His constant attempts to avoid appearing phony is revealed in his rejection of certain words and phrases which he considers to be pretentious: 'grand', 'little girls' room', 'traveling incognito'. His awareness of the wider social significance of the way people express themselves is seen in his response to the prostitute's use of the childish phrase, 'Like fun you are.' Holden comments that it was odd to hear a prostitute using the idiom of a small child.

A few other aspects of Holden's speech deserve particular comment. Among the most obvious of these is his characteristically juvenile habit of wild exaggeration as when he says that Ackley probably looked at Sally Hayes's photograph about five thousand times or that Mrs Antolini was almost sixty years older than her husband. He often uses overstatement for ironic effect as when Ackley refuses to let him sleep in Ely's bed and he tells Ackley, in a mocking tone, that he is a truly wonderful and noble human being. Such exchanges are very funny; however, Holden's ironic humour is usually a defence against depression and despair.

But of all the ways in which Holden uses American-English to describe himself and his world, the word 'phony' is the most significant in his analysis. It is used innumerable times throughout the story to characterise almost every aspect of New York life and the people who live there. 'Phony' means all that is superficial, dishonest, shoddy or insincere in the way people live and behave towards one another. It is indicative of Holden's view of his situation that this one word becomes his habitual response to an environment and culture that he finds intolerable.

Salinger's achievement in the creation of his central character and narrator lies, finally, in the fact that we experience the story as a spoken account rather than as a written document. We always hear Holden's voice with its characteristic tone and idiom. The narrative gives the impression of being a spontaneous outpouring of personal experience without any preordained plan or shape. That this is so is, perhaps, the best testimony to the artistic skill of the creator of one of the most memorable characters in modern fiction.

Themes

Place and alienation

There are three locations in *The Catcher in the Rye*: Pencey Prep, located a short train ride from New York; the city itself where most of the events of the story take place; the institution outside Hollywood in which Holden is recovering as he narrates his experiences. It is useful to view these three places as a composite image of American society in the postwar years.

Pencey, probably based upon Salinger's memories of Valley Forge Military Academy, is an institution that prepares the sons of the middle-classes for their roles as future businessmen, educators or administrators. Its stated image as an idealised community masks its system of cliques that is anathema to Holden's kind of individuality.

When Holden escapes from the school he is, like Huckleberry Finn, 'lighting out for the territory' in that old American tradition of taking to the road. The individual who is unable to live within the physical and the moral constraints of society dates back to Colonial days and the creation of myths of the frontier. These myths have been updated by later generations as in innumerable Western movies, some of the most memorable being almost contemporaneous with Salinger's novel: *High Noon* (1952), *Shane* (1953), *The Searchers* (1956). The a-social type who takes to the road became an icon for the 1960s; popularised for that generation by Jack Kerouac's novel, *On the Road* (1957) and given wide appeal in much popular culture, in particular the film *Easy Rider* (1969).

The city in which Holden wanders for three days is recognisably the New York of the late 1940s. The reader's sense of an actual city is intensified by the fact that we observe things through the eyes of an intelligent, sensitive observer as he roams in order to fill in the time on his hands. What he sees and experiences captures New York in the age before television dominated American culture: Broadway, Radio City Music Hall, the long queues for the cinemas, Ernie's sleazy nightclub, the 'guys' and their 'dates' as they go for a night on the town. It is a culture given over to entertainment and diversion in which the presiding spirit, to Holden's intense annoyance, is imported from Hollywood.

The fact that he has nothing to do and goes from place to place, more or less on impulse, creates a vivid sense of the vastness of the city as well as the feeling of isolation caused by being surrounded by thousands who are indifferent to his presence. Holden often admits to his acute sense of loneliness among so many people; the sense of his isolation is emphasised by his numerous unsuccessful telephone calls. At one point in the story he imagines living in the country alone as being preferable to the city. On his date with Sally (Chapter 17) he expresses his detestation of the traffic, the Lunts, and New York life in general. He becomes particularly upset by the city's ubiquitous graffiti and only finds peace and refuge in the museum where everything is still and silent.

The view that urban life is alien to man's true nature has been deeply planted in the American psyche since the frontier began to give way to the expanding towns and cities of the nineteenth century. It has found continuous and varied expression in literature, the visual arts and in films since the beginning of motion pictures. In this respect *The Catcher in the Rye* reinterprets traditional values, assumptions and conventions for its own time.

Holden's dream of escape, peace and silence in a cabin beside the wood in the wilderness reflects that need for space and air that was so much a part of frontier idealism. Mark Twain's *Huckleberry Finn* is the novel that has given this its most complex expression. Twain's story is, however, deeply pessimistic; it suggests that true freedom and integrity are available only outside human society, in close communion with the natural world. Salinger's novel is less optimistic about the possibility of achieving and maintaining individuality. Huck Finn had the great Mississippi river, a raft and a devoted companion in Jim, the runaway slave. Holden's world is more crowded, urbanised and complex. There is less space in which to move and less fresh air to breathe. The simple stratagem of escaping on a raft is no longer possible by the middle of the twentieth century. Society in *The Catcher in the Rye* is all-pervasive; it is partly because he feels that there is no real escape from a world that is becoming increasingly regimented and mass-produced that Holden suffers his breakdown. Everywhere he goes he sees the reduction of each individual's spirit to a common, banal sameness. Each of the schools that he attends force their pupils to conform to rigid social and academic standards. Even those with real talent like D.B. and Mr Antolini are seduced by the easy rewards of a mass culture. It is a world ruled by phoniness in which childish innocence is under continual threat and true self-reliance results in forms of dislocation or, as in the case of James Castle (Chapter 22), in death. Holden's fantasy of being the catcher of childhood innocence is as pathetic and futile as it is noble.

Teenage identity

On a more mundane level, if we ask why Holden feels a sense of alienation, we have to remember that although the existence of 'adolescence' was acknowledged, the concept of teenagers as a distinct social group, with its own icons and rebellious culture expressed in music, films and fashion, simply did not exist during Salinger's own teenage years in the 1930s and only emerged in the 1950s when it became symbolically identified with Rock 'n Roll. Before then, the teenager felt a sense of isolation – alienation even – in a society that catered for children up to school-leaving age, and adults thereafter.

Holden's sense of alienation from such a society is admirably highlighted in *The Catcher in the Rye*, and at the time of its original publication was seen by teenagers as recognising their plight. Holden's position caught in this uncertain world between childhood and adulthood, no longer truly belonging to childhood yet still attracted by its security (in the form of his young sister's confident, cosy world where she has a definite sense of identity), and as yet unaccepted by the adult world is an essential element of the book's poignant humour.

Holden's train journey, his directionless wanderings around New York and sojourn in a hotel might all be interpreted as symbolic of the no-man's-land between the childhood world of school, which he had rejected, and the adult world of his parents which he also rejects.

We witness his, as yet unsuccessful, attempts at adulthood being put down by the scathing remarks of Faith Cavendish (Chapter 9), by the barman (Chapter 10), the cab-driver (Chapter 12), by the prostitute (Chapter 13), the hall porter (Chapter 14) and Carl Luce (Chapter 18), for example.

Holden's wish to re-enter the world of childhood is expressed when he buys his small sister the record of 'Little Shirley Beans', a child's song recorded by the blues singer Estelle Fletcher (Chapter 16), and its shattering later in the book is symbolic of his inability to do so. His thoughts about the 'catcher in the rye' also express nostalgia for the innocent world of childhood.

Philosophical/religious aspects

Holden is not religious in the conventional sense of going regularly to a place of worship or following strict principles of behaviour. In fact, since the death of his brother, he cannot accept traditional faith. His closest contact with organised religion occurs in Chapter 15 when he meets two nuns at Grand Central Station and gives them a ten-dollar donation at a point when he is running short of money. The episode is typical of what could be called Holden's practical Christianity. He is interested in the nuns only insofar as they are good women and not as representatives of the Roman Catholic church. As in this episode, his impulse is always to do some practical good rather than to preach abstract virtue. His most striking characteristic is a detestation of empty gestures and insincere rhetoric, all of which come under his collective description of phoniness.

In Chapter 14 he admits to liking Jesus but is irritated by his disciples and by most of the biblical narrative. Similarly, he makes a generous donation to the nuns but says that he dislikes ministers (because of their elevated and unnatural language). In many respects there is much in Holden's behaviour that recalls the life of Christ. This is most obvious in his concern for the weak and vulnerable. In Chapter 14, for instance, he worries about Jane Gallagher's welfare on her date with Stradlater and throughout the story he is concerned for the wellbeing of children. In Holden's preoccupation with the protection of their innocence we recall Christ's injunction, 'suffer little children to come unto me' and his warning to those who might corrupt children that it would be better for them to have a millstone tied round their necks and be cast into the sea. In Holden's fantasy of himself as the catcher in the rye (Chapter 22) there is a distinct resemblance to the pious image of Jesus Christ in many popular reproductions, which depicts him surrounded by imploring, white-clad boys and girls. Holden's familiar and affectionate allusion to 'Old Jesus' who would have been nauseated by the sentimental Christmas show (Chapter 18) suggests that Salinger's identification of his young hero with Christ was more than a casual one.

Paradoxically, Holden's Christ-like aspects serve to emphasise the post-Christian condition of contemporary American life. The New York of the novel is a city of sleaze and crime that is dominated by the products of the new mass culture. In these surroundings Holden is a pathetic figure of defeat rather than a transcendent saviour. The closest that he comes to a vision of Paradise is the model of an Eskimo fishing in the museum.

This is a world that is spiritually diminished; it is a post-industrial culture in which family structures appear to have almost vanished to be replaced by teenage peer groups and the pervasive influence of Hollywood. As a symbol of a generation Holden cuts a sad, lonely figure. One of the novel's most lasting impressions is of older generations having withdrawn, leaving the central character and his contemporaries alone in a difficult and dangerous world. In this sense it is possible to see in *The Catcher in the Rye* an American counterpart to the existentialist texts of such European writers as Jean-Paul Sartre (1905–80) and Albert Camus (1913–60).

Characters

Holden Caulfield

Holden Caulfield is both the narrator and the main character in the novel. The whole book is his story and all of the other characters are presented to us as he sees them. Although he sets out to tell the reader of his experiences over a period of only a few days, his habit of digressing leads him to give a very full account of his background and previous history.

Holden is seventeen years old and he begins his narrative by recounting his doings during his final days at Pencey, a preparatory school near New York. He has been expelled because of his poor school record and faces the prospect of having to explain his failure to his parents when he returns to New York for the Christmas vacation. His opening words are, apparently, off-hand and he informs the reader, in a seemingly casual manner, that he will tell the reader about the crazy events that took place last Christmas before he became ill and had to go away to recover.

From time to time he gives the reader an assessment of himself. He admits that he is one of the greatest liars ever and agrees with Carl Luce that he has an immature mind. However, it is in his accounts of the many people with whom he comes into contact that we get the clearest insights into his character.

Holden has many positive virtues. He is kind and willing to help others. For instance, he lends Ackley his scissors and writes Stradlater's essay for him. He is naturally generous and considerate of people's feelings. On the train to New York he lies to a Pencey pupil's mother about her son's popularity at school in order to make her happy. He gives two nuns ten dollars for charity even though he is running short of money for his own use. He asks the lonely Ackley to go to the cinema in spite of the fact that he dislikes his company.

It is Holden's generosity and sensitivity that lie at the root of his war with the world and lead to his eventual breakdown. Everywhere that he goes he sees signs of man's shortcomings which offend his high, if vague, ideals. Sometimes he witnesses depravity and cruelty as in his encounter with the prostitute and her pimp. But more often he is concerned with the pretentiousness and dishonesty that he detects in the behaviour of so many people. These constitute the phonies who populate the novel. Holden sees signs of phoniness in almost every area of life. He says, for example, that he left Elkton Hills school because he was surrounded by phonies. He compares the genuine goodness of the nuns with the insincere charitable works of his aunt who would only go around collecting with a basket if everyone admired her for being so charitable. His hatred of the American film industry is based on a belief that the movies give an unreal picture of life; they create a vision of the world that is essentially 'phony'. At various times throughout the novel he expresses his detestation for Hollywood and the ruinous films made there. In fact the addiction of the American public to the cinema as a major form of entertainment is, for Holden, symbolic of society's cultural and spiritual shortcomings.

Holden feels that society inevitably crushes the best in the individual. When he bids farewell to the escort of his brother's former girlfriend in the nightclub, he explains his own 'phony' behaviour saying that he always engages in polite, social exchanges because it's necessary in order to get by in society. Nevertheless, Holden's almost neurotic dislike of everything he describes has led many critics to argue that Salinger's view of society is seriously unbalanced and that his heroes are those made mad by their fear of social realities.* However, this is a criticism of which Salinger is himself aware. Indeed Phoebe accuses Holden of being totally negative towards almost everything in his life. When she challenges him to name something he does like he can only think of the two nuns and James Castle, each of whom is distinguished by their exceptional lives. The nuns have renounced the world and James Castle committed suicide because he was bullied at school.

Holden's deep fear of coming to terms with the adult world is revealed in his love of children and in his idealisation of the state of childhood. Children, particularly his sister, Phoebe, are the only people with whom he can make any genuine human contact. He lives with the memory of his dead brother, Allie, who died when he was very young. Holden remembers that on the night he died he became violent with frustration and broke all the windows in the garage with his bare hands. The innocence of children is something that Holden would love to preserve. When a child becomes an adult he loses the purity of youth and is corrupted by the world of grown-ups. It is this belief that explains his fantasy of playing the catcher in the rye. To stop the inevitable 'fall' of children into adulthood is Holden's idealistic dream. He imagines himself as the catcher in the rye whose single task it is to stop children falling over the edge of a cliff. He confesses that the reader may think that this fantasy is mad but he can't help it.

Holden's horror at the prospect of having to face an unattractive future in an uncongenial society explains the strong conservative streak in his nature. He is attracted to the natural history museum because it contains examples of life which have been frozen at a moment in time and, consequently, will never change. He likes the carousels in the park because they never vary the music that they play. His deep love for Allie is due, in a large part, to the fact that the dead boy will always be eleven years old in his memory and, therefore, can never be corrupted by the world.

Holden Caulfield is a lonely character whose sense of isolation is

*See, for example, Jack Ludwig's comments in *Recent American Novelists*, Minneapolis, 1962, pp. 28–30.

caused by an inability to adjust to life's inevitable limitations. He is unable to make the kind of compromises that are necessary in order to make the harsher realities of existence at least tolerable, especially urban life in twentieth-century America. The novelist, Philip Roth (*b.* 1933), had the following to say about this very situation and the difficulty that it poses for creative artists, such as Salinger and himself. He wrote:

> The American writer in the middle of the twentieth century has his hands full in trying to describe and then to make credible much of the American reality. It stupefies, it sickens, it infuriates, and finally it is even a kind of embarrassment to one's own meager imagination. The actuality is continually outdoing our talents, and the culture tosses up figures almost daily that are the envy of any novelist.*

In his portrayal of Holden Caulfield, Salinger created a character whose almost abnormal sensitivity would not allow him to adjust to what Roth referred to as 'the American reality.' Like the central character in a famous novel by Nathanael West (1902–40), *Miss Lonelyhearts* (1933), a work which has much in common with *The Catcher in the Rye*, Holden is crushed by his inability to ignore all or even most of what he finds amiss in the world about him. To argue that *The Catcher in the Rye* gives a distorted view of American life is to miss the point of the novel. Salinger did not set out to write a sociological or historical study of society. His intention was to show us the world through the eyes of a very unusual teenager, and if we are to judge his achievement fairly we must always bear in mind the singular and limited perspective of the narrator.

This limitation is very apparent when we come to consider the other characters in the book. With the possible exception of Phoebe, they are all one-dimensional figures. Each is little more than an example of some single aspect of human behaviour. This, of course, is not a shortcoming on the part of the author. It is rather an inevitable result of the kind of novel he wanted to write. It is Holden who narrates the story and he is chiefly concerned with telling the reader about himself. His account of all the other characters is, therefore, limited to the effect that they have upon his state of mind. He is rarely concerned with any of them for their own intrinsic interest and, consequently, his accounts are often fleeting and superficial. His usual practice is simply to allot each one of them to either the ranks of the phonies or those of the non-phonies.

Robert Ackley

Ackley is a student at Pencey school. He is an unattractive boy who often infuriates Holden by his irritating habits. It is in his relationship with

*Quoted in Alfred Kazin, *Bright Book of Life*, Secker and Warburg, London, 1974, p. 147.

Ackley that we see some of Holden's most admirable qualities, especially his generosity and his imaginative sympathy for the underdog.

Ward Stradlater

Stradlater is Holden's roommate at Pencey. He is a handsome boy who is very mature for his age. Holden admires his social manners and his ability to get on with girls. However, Stradlater tends to exploit people and Holden becomes angry when he suspects that Stradlater has taken advantage of Jane Gallagher.

Allie Caulfield

Allie was Holden's younger brother who died at the age of eleven. Although he never actually appears in person, his memory is always fresh in Holden's mind as a perfect example of kindness, good humour and generosity.

Phoebe Caulfield

Phoebe is Holden's ten-year-old sister. She is the only person with whom he is capable of sustaining a close relationship. At the beginning of Chapter 10 he describes her as a very clever ten-year-old who always gets A grades at school. She is skinny with short red hair that reminds him of Allie's. Holden insists that the reader would like her because she is quick on the uptake and very affectionate, perhaps too much so for her own good.

This assessment of the little girl is borne out by her subsequent behaviour. She shows a degree of maturity and insight well beyond her years in her reaction to Holden's announcement that he has been expelled from school. Her annoyance with her brother, however, is shortlived, and she shows her loyalty by offering to run away with him.

D. B. Caulfield

D.B. is Holden's elder brother who earns his living as a scriptwriter in Hollywood. According to Holden he is a 'prostitute' who has sold his true creative talents for the easy money of the film industry.

Mr Antolini

Antolini was Holden's English teacher at Elkton Hills school. He was one of the very few adults in whom Holden had any confidence. He offers Holden a bed in his flat when the boy has nowhere else to go. But this encounter turns out badly. Holden senses that Antolini has married his wife for her money and, instead of trying to understand Holden's problems, he offers some platitudinous advice on how to behave in the future. Holden runs away from the flat when he suspects that Antolini is making a sexual advance towards him. However, Holden later feels that he may have misjudged Antolini and he remembers that he wasn't annoyed that Holden had telephoned him so late at night and that he told him to come over straightaway. He also remembers the good advice Antolini gave him about his intellectual development and that he was the only teacher to take an interest in James Castle. This reflection is one of the few occasions when Holden shows a mature insight into the complex nature of another character.

Minor characters

Many of the characters in *The Catcher in the Rye* are little more than names that crop up from time to time in Holden's story. They have no life beyond his fleeting references to them. His parents and his aunt are wealthy middle-class people who never appear in person in the tale. Holden also refers to a number of his former teachers, Mr Spencer, Miss Aigletinger and Mr Vinson, as well as to several former school friends including Mal Brossard, Ely and James Castle, the young boy who killed himself. Carl Luce was a fellow student of Holden's at Whooton school and is currently studying at Columbia University. He joins Holden for a drink in the Wicker Bar (Chapter 19), but has little patience with the younger man's childish questions about sex.

Holden introduces two of his girlfriends into the story. Sally Hayes he refers to as an arch-phony, but Jane Gallagher is a more interesting and complex girl who has a troubled home background.

Holden's first experience of the seedier side of New York life occurs in his encounter with Sunny, the prostitute, and her pimp, Maurice, in the Edmont hotel. Both of these characters are vividly drawn and Salinger shows great skill in handling the dialogue in the chapters (13 and 14) in which these characters appear.

A few other characters are mentioned by Holden, but these are of so little consequence in the story that they require no special comment.

Part 4

Hints for study

Studying *The Catcher in the Rye*

The best way to study *The Catcher in the Rye* is:

(1) To read the novel through without reference to the summaries or to the commentary in these notes. You should, however, use the glossaries after each summary and supplement these with a good dictionary such as *The Concise Oxford Dictionary*. It is also advisable to make your own synopsis of each chapter as you read it. This will help you to retain the story in greater detail.

(2) Having read the book in the above way, to reread it, consulting the summaries in Part 2 on each chapter as you go along and making your own more detailed notes at the same time.

(3) To study the critical commentary in Part 3. It is advisable to reread the episodes referred to or discussed in detail in this section.

For convenience we can divide the major points for detailed study into the following categories, although it should be remembered that there is a good deal of overlapping in such divisions and a discussion of any one of these may involve reference to one or more of the others:

Characters – Characterisation

Consider the part played by each of the characters in the story, their chief characteristics (that is, good, evil, wise, foolish, hypocritical, humorous, etc.) and examine the way they interrelate with the other characters as well as the way they are portrayed by the author. Are they fully rounded portraits or are they rather one-dimensional; would you say they are believable as characters? Does the course of events see them develop at all and does the reader's opinion of them alter over time?

The plot

See how the story is organised in terms of the things that take place and the way in which these events work out in the conclusion. You might think about whether the ending is satisfying or not and, if not, why not. In considering the plot you should be able to discuss the relevance of any single episode to the overall development of the story.

Narrative

Look at the way the story is told and consider how this helps our understanding of characters and events. What effect do Holden's digressions have? Are they confusing or enlightening? Of course, in *The Catcher in the Rye* any consideration of the narrative will involve an assessment of Holden who tells the story.

Sample questions

(1) Write a critical description of Holden Caulfield.
(2) Discuss the use of language in *The Catcher in the Rye.*
(3) Discuss Salinger's characterisation in the novel.
(4) What functions do the minor characters have in the story?
(5) *The Catcher in the Rye* is a novel about growing up. Discuss.
(6) Consider the plot of *The Catcher in the Rye.*
(7) Write an account of the view of American society in *The Catcher in the Rye.*
(8) What part does religion play in the novel?
(9) Is *The Catcher in the Rye* a pessimistic book?
(10) Examine the novel's humour.

Sample answers

Arrangement of material in answering questions – some examples:
(1) Make your central points at the opening of your essay.
(2) Try to devote a single paragraph to the development of each point.
(3) Illustrate your answer by referring to specific scenes in the novel, or, if relevant, by suitable quotations. You may not remember exactly the words used in the text but a concise and accurate paraphrase will do instead.
(4) Try to write as simply as possible and avoid writing long sentences. Keep to the point in your answers and avoid the temptation of discussing aspects of the work which have nothing to do with the question just to show you know those aspects.
(5) Summarise the main points in a succinct concluding paragraph.

The following is intended to give you some idea of how you could formulate your answers when writing either for coursework or for an exam.

(1) Write a critical description of Holden Caulfield

The Catcher in the Rye is Holden Caulfield's story. He is the main character and narrator, and all of the other characters are presented to us through his eyes.

He sets out to tell the reader about the crazy events that he experienced last Christmas just before he had a breakdown and had to come to a clinic in order to convalesce. Although he intends to tell the reader of his experiences over a period of only a few days his habit of digressing leads him to give a very full account of his background and previous history.

Holden is seventeen years old, and he begins his story by recounting his experiences of the final day at Pencey, a preparatory school near New York. He has been expelled because of his poor school record and faces the unpleasant prospect of having to explain his failure to his parents when he returns home to New York for the vacation.

Occasionally Holden gives the reader an assessment of himself. He admits that he is a terrific liar and agrees with Carl Luce that he is immature. However, it is in his accounts of the people whom he meets that we get the clearest insights into his character. Holden has many positive virtues. He is kind and willing to help. For example, he writes an essay for Stradlater and lends Ackley his scissors. He is naturally generous and considerate of the feelings of others. He lies to the mother of a Pencey pupil about her son's popularity at school in order to protect her maternal feelings. He gives the two nuns ten dollars for charity even though he has little money left for his own use. He invites the lonely Ackley to join him on an outing in spite of the fact that he dislikes his company.

Ironically, it is this generosity and sensitivity that cause many of Holden's personal problems. He is always aware of human shortcomings which offend his high ideals. Sometimes he witnesses depravity and cruelty as in his encounter with the prostitute and her pimp at the Edmont hotel. But more often he is conscious of the dishonesty and pretensions that govern the behaviour of so many people. These are the 'phonies' so often encountered by Holden. He sees signs of phoniness in almost every area of life. He tells us that he left his former school, Elkton Hills, because he was surrounded by phonies. He hates the cinema because it offers a phony view of real life. In Holden's estimation few people are wholly genuine. The two nuns, whom he meets at Grand Central Station, get his approval because their way of life is totally devoted to the welfare of others. He likes small children because they have not been corrupted by the world and his fantastic desire to be 'the catcher in the rye' reflects his wish to preserve their innocence. He would like to stop their growth into adulthood with its inevitable destruction of personal integrity.

Holden feels that society crushes the best in the individual. For instance, when he says goodbye to the naval officer who accompanies D.B.'s former girlfriend at the nightclub he confesses that his 'Glad to have met you' was insincere and adds that you have to say such things if you want to survive.

However, Holden's almost neurotic dislike of everything he describes has led many readers to argue that Salinger's view of society is unbalanced and that his central character has been driven insane by his fear of the world. But the author himself was surely aware of this in writing the novel. When, for example, Phoebe accuses Holden of not liking a single thing he finds it difficult to defend himself against this charge. He can only think of his regard for the nuns and for James Castle, all of whom lead, or have led, exceptional lives. The nuns have given up the good things of life for God and James Castle committed suicide because he was bullied at school.

Certainly Holden Caulfield is not a 'normal' character. But it is his exceptional qualities that make him such a memorable one. He is a lonely figure whose isolation from society is caused by an inability to adjust to life's inevitable limitations. Holden is unable to make the kind of compromises that are necessary in order to make existence tolerable in twentieth-century America. The pressures that led to his stay in a psychiatric clinic are a measure of his self-destructive idealism.

(3) Discuss Salinger's characterisation in the novel

The character of Holden Caulfield dominates the novel. He narrates the story of his experiences and, consequently, we see people and events through his eyes. Holden is primarily concerned to explain why he is in a psychiatric clinic. The story is, therefore, built around one character. He introduces the reader to a wide variety of people in the course of his tale, but their existence is of significance only in so far as it affects Holden.

By the time we get to the end of the story we have gained a very full and detailed impression of Holden and of the variety of pressures that led to his illness. However, with very few exceptions, none of the other characters are portrayed in any real detail. Most of them are used as examples of ways of life or behaviour that are either 'phony' or sincere. They have no substantial existence outside the categories in which the narrator places them.

A few examples will illustrate this point. Ackley, for instance, figures largely in the early chapters of the novel. He is an unattractive boy who displays a variety of irritating habits. No one likes Ackley and only Holden is willing to make any friendly gestures towards him. As a character he is a 'stock' schoolboy 'type' and there is no attempt made to probe into his character in order to explain why he is the person he is. His role is simply to reveal an aspect of Pencey that helped to make the school unbearable for Holden. Much the same can be said about the character of Stradlater. He is a very different 'type' from Ackley, but there is no deep exploration of his true personality in the novel. He, too, is of significance only in so far as he acts as a further factor in Holden's gradual alienation from society. The same point can be made about several other characters. For example, the nuns whom Holden meets at the station assume a symbolic importance for him simply because, on the surface, they are religious women whose lives are dedicated to the service of others. We learn nothing of their real selves beyond the most superficial details revealed in Holden's conversation with them over breakfast.

Many of the characters are little more than names mentioned by Holden from time to time as examples of sincerity or phoniness. Several of his former teachers fall into this category. So, too, does Holden's aunt whom he contrasts unfavourably with the nuns. There are, however, a few exceptions to this rule. Mr Antolini, Holden's former English teacher, appears in only one chapter. Yet, even in this brief dramatic episode, we get some insight into his make-up and see what pressures have made him into the man he has become. He is one of the few characters who enjoy a life outside Holden's rigid categories. The other obvious exception is, of course, Holden's young sister, Phoebe. For most of the novel we see her through her brother's idealised reminiscences of her. However, in those scenes towards the end of the novel when she appears in person, she shows herself to be a character of more complexity than Holden would have the reader believe. In fact she reveals herself to be her brother's most rigorous critic as well as his greatest admirer.

Yet, the fact that most of the characters lack the complexity of Phoebe is not a shortcoming on the part of the author. It is, rather, an inevitable result of the kind of book he wanted to write. Salinger attempted to portray the mind and personality of a very unusual adolescent and, consequently, characterisation was dictated by his need to allow our view of most of the people in the story to be revealed to us through Holden's idiosyncratic perceptions of them.

(6) Consider the plot of *The Catcher in the Rye*

Plot can be defined as the organisation of dramatic action in which character and theme are revealed. The plot of *The Catcher in the Rye* is very simple, in keeping with the author's intention of allowing Holden to reveal his character to the reader. The events narrated in the story take place over a period of only four days.

(1) Chapters 1–7 relate the events at Pencey school prior to Holden's early departure.
(2) Chapters 8–25 take place in New York City.
(3) Chapter 26, the short epilogue to the novel, sees Holden in a psychiatric clinic. We learn that it is here that he has composed this account of his experiences.

However, the narrative is not strictly chronological, as the above summary might suggest. Although Holden sets out to tell what happened over a very short period of time, he often digresses and recounts many episodes from his past life. Therefore, instead of learning about a single episode in his experience, we get a fairly comprehensive and detailed account of his history. To achieve this Salinger employs a device known as 'flashback'. In this kind of narration the line of the story is apparently dictated by the teller's random stream of associations and memories. One fact or detail brings another similar or associated incident to mind so that the narrator tends to wander from the main point of his story, as we all do in our everyday conversations.

The actual dramatic events that constitute the novel's plot are dictated by the narrative method. Occurrences take place in a seemingly arbitrary way as Holden wanders around New York in an attempt to make some kind of human contact to ease his 'lonesomeness'. These episodic chapters show the author employing one of the oldest of all dramatic narrative devices, the 'picaresque'. This kind of loose structure was well suited to Salinger's purpose in writing the novel. It allowed him to introduce a wide variety of characters into the story. He could let Holden come into contact with various people without sacrificing the realism of the story as any encounter is at least possible on a three-day ramble around a large city. Furthermore, this freedom suited the author's wider intentions. He wanted to create an impression of the impersonality of life in a place like New York for a young person. This freedom to allow Holden to meet a broad cross-section of humanity was fundamental to the book's success.

(7) Write an account of the view of American society in *The Catcher in the Rye*

When discussing the artist's view of the world we must always be careful to keep in mind that the work of art is only one person's vision of reality. No matter how realistic the portrayal of actual places or events may appear to be, we must remember that the hand of its creator lies behind it, shaping and conditioning our perceptions and understanding.

The Catcher in the Rye is a case in point. Salinger has placed his hero in an historically defined *milieu*. The city is New York and the time is around the late 1940s. The fate of the central character is largely brought about by the current values and pressures that he sees as the distinctive characteristics of his culture. Holden Caulfield's disillusioned view of his world is a very persuasive one and, no doubt, it does make some valid criticisms of the real America of the day. But, in analysing that view, we must be wary of making too easy and superficial an identification with historical realities.

Holden's wanderings around New York create a very vivid impression of the size of the city and the feeling of isolation caused by being surrounded by so many people who are totally careless of anyone's welfare except their own. In his encounters with taxi drivers and bar attendants, for example, he experiences a professional indifference to his personal existence and a lack of curiosity about the world in which they live. This boorish mindlessness seems to be a characteristic of most people's lives. When he meets the three girls from Seattle in the hotel bar he becomes depressed to learn that they are prepared to get up early next morning in order to see the first show at Radio City Music Hall. Holden regards the addiction of so many people to this kind of mass-culture as a symptom of the imaginative poverty of their lives. The long cinema queues on Broadway annoy and depress him. He sees this as the most obvious example of New York's spiritual sterility and is angry that his brother, D.B., is 'prostituting' his literary talents by writing film scripts in Hollywood.

The malaise that Holden finds prevalent in society is also reflected in his account of Pencey and the other schools which he has attended. Each of these institutions is characterised by rigid and unimaginative social and academic values. They are unwilling to accommodate true individuality and sensitivity. Those who will not conform to their fixed standards are ostracised, like Holden, or are driven to despair, as in the case of James Castle. Stradlater is a typical product of such a limited education. When Holden presents him with the 'descriptive' essay which Stradlater was unable to write himself, he rejects it on the grounds that it doesn't exactly fit the class teacher's prescriptions. Holden's account of the 'oral expression' class in Chapter 24 is a fine example of a form of education that is totally lacking in the imagination and flexibility necessary to cater for the needs of the most inventive pupils. In the novel the school system faithfully reflects the values of society at large as experienced by Holden.

Holden's eventual nervous breakdown is a result of his inability to adapt himself to the aspirations and expectations of American society. His own inner impulses and needs always run counter to the wishes of his parents, schoolfriends and teachers. He can only find consolation in the innocent company of children. In this respect he is a very representative figure in twentieth-century fiction: the anti-hero who is always at odds with an uncongenial society.

Part 5

Suggestions for further reading

The text

SALINGER, J. D.: *The Catcher in the Rye*. Little, Brown, Boston, 1951. Reprinted in its original form by Penguin Books, Harmondsworth, 1994.

Other work by the author

Raise High the Roof Beam, Carpenters and Seymour: An Introduction. Penguin Books, Harmondsworth, 1964.

Critical works on J. D. Salinger

GWYNN, FREDERICK L. and BLOTNER, JOSEPH L.: *The Fiction of J. D. Salinger*. University of Pittsburgh Press, Pittsburgh, 1958.

GRUNWALD, HENRY ANATOLE (ED.): *Salinger: A Critical and Personal Portrait*. Peter Owen, London, 1962.

HAMILTON, IAN: *In Search of J. D. Salinger*. New York: Random House, 1988 and London: Minerva, 1989.

General Studies of Modern American Fiction

BAUMBACH, JONATHAN: *The Landscapes of Nightmare: Studies in the Contemporary American Novel.* New York University Press, New York, 1965.

BRADBURY, MALCOLM: *The Modern American Novel*. New York: Oxford University Press, 1984.

KAZIN, ALFRED: *Bright Book of Life: American Novelists and Storytellers from Hemingway to Mailer*. Secker and Warburg, London, 1974.

LUDWIG, JACK: *Recent American Novelists*. (University of Minnesota Pamphlets on American Writers, No. 22) University of Minnesota Press, Minneapolis, 1962.

TANNER, TONY: *City of Words: American Fiction 1950–70*. Jonathan Cape, London, 1971.

The author of these notes

BRIAN DONNELLY was educated at the University of Essex. He was lecturer in English literature at the University of Aarhus, Denmark from 1972 to 1976. He was a visiting professor at Rutgers University, New Jersey from 1981 to 1983, and head of the English Department at Carysfort College, Dublin from 1983 until 1987. Since 1987 he has been a senior lecturer in English and Anglo-Irish literature at University College, Dublin. He has published widely on English, Anglo-Irish and American literature.